Correct Dress
for Riders

British Library Cataloguing in Publication Data
A catalogue record for this book is available from the British Library.

ISBN 0-900226-47-1

Text Judith Draper
Design and Setting Hugh Johnson
Photographs Hugh Pinney, Jane O' Dell, Ian Shaw, Anthony Reynolds
Illustrations by Maggie Raynor

The Pony Club acknowledge with thanks the help given in providing equipment by
Horsesense and Townfield Saddlery

Contents

Introduction

Riding clothes, like all other sportswear, are based on practical design combined with a certain amount of fashion. They have evolved over a period of several thousand years, during which time man has depended on the horse for transport, war and, relatively recently, leisure activities.

The design of riding clothes has changed, and no doubt will continue to change, according to the uses to which horses are put. It has always been governed by available materials and, to a certain extent, by climate. The ancient Egyptians and Greeks rode in flimsy garments which reflected their everyday dress in a warm climate. Bare legs probably gave as good a grip as anything in those pre-saddle days.

On the other hand, remarkably well preserved objects found in the frozen burial mounds at Pazyrik in the High Altai Mountains show that the nomadic Siberian horseman of 2,500 years ago wore a tunic over trousers tucked into short, pliable boots which were strapped at the ankle. This style of clothing afforded maximum protection from the extremes of the northern winters and is not a million miles from today's basic riding gear.

Nor is there anything new in the concept of protective wear. Mounted warriors, from the Assyrians onwards, soon saw the sense in protecting their heads with helmets, while 'body protectors' over the centuries took the form of everything from metal-covered felt or leather garments to linked chain mail and entire suits of metal armour. Such clothing, of course, was aimed at protecting the rider from enemy weapons, whereas today it is used to guard against injury in the event of a fall.

However, with the exception of the suit of armour, the comfort and mobility of the rider have generally been the prime considerations, with fashion a secondary but ever present factor. This can be seen in the elaborate decorative work adorning some of the finest suits of armour and the flamboyant costumes worn for hunting and tournaments from the Middle Ages onwards.

During the last few centuries extraneous decoration has largely been pared away, just as it has in everyday dress, leaving today's participant in competitive horse sports with the practical and, mostly, elegant attire based on breeches or jodhpurs (a style brought to the west from India) and boots, shirt, jacket and hard hat.

Using that as a basis, the different modern-day horse sports have developed their own variations. The purpose of this book is to outline the most suitable type of dress for each equestrian activity and to give the current requirements according to the rules of each sport.

Every form of horsemanship, from riding in an indoor school or hacking on today's increasingly overcrowded roads to jumping fixed obstacles at speed, involves a certain degree of danger. Accordingly, safety is given priority in this book. Great strides have been made in recent years in the production of safer headgear and body protectors, as well as high visibility garments for use when riding in traffic. Everyone who rides, at whatever level, is urged to wear, at all times, the very best safety gear available.

- **Remember that safety standards are constantly being improved. Riders are advised to keep up to date with the latest developments and to change their equipment, as necessary, to take advantage of improvements in protection.**

- **Rules are constantly being amended and riders should always check the current rulebook of their chosen sport before setting out to compete.**

Abbreviations:

AHSA:	American House Shows Association.
ASTM:	American Society for Testing and Materials.
BETA:	British Equestrian Trade Association.
BHS:	British Horse Society.
BHTA:	British Horse Trials Association.
BS:	British Standards.
BSEN:	Harmonised European Standard
BSPS:	British Show Pony Society.
BSJA:	British Show Jumping Association.
CE	Communauté Européenne
EN	Harmonised European Standard
FEI:	Fédération Equestre International
PAS:	Product Approval Specification.
SEL:	Safety Equipment Institute.
USET:	United States Equestrian Team.

1
Safety First

However well schooled the horse or pony and however skilful the rider, there is no getting away from the fact that riding is a risk sport and everyone is going to fall off at some time. Anyone who falls from a height of several feet, particularly at speed, stands a chance of injuring some part of their body. The rider's head is particularly vulnerable, not only to the impact of a fall but also, sometimes, to collision with objects such as overhanging branches. If you do fall off, you might hit your head on a fence pole or sharp stone, or you might be dragged along or be kicked or trodden on by the horse. It is, therefore, irresponsible not to wear the best available protective headgear at all times when mounted. Remember, to, that you can be equally at risk when lungeing, long-reining, or even just leading a horse, especially an unpredictable or young one.

Hats

It doesn't take a large, visible wound to cause brain damage. The effects of a blow that leaves only a small wound, or perhaps no visible wound at all, can be far-reaching, as the real trouble may be inside the skull rather than on the outside. We only have one brain and it can't be repaired, so it makes sense to protect it. Brain damage will seriously affect not only your own quality of life but that of your family and other people who would have to look after you, so while you might think, I don't want to wear a hat — it's my own problem if I get hurt, remember you have a responsibility towards others. Also, remember that if you're under 14 years old the law says you must wear an approved standard hat when riding on a public highway.

Hats are designed to minimise the risk of brain injury by absorbing as much impact as possible. Think of your brain as being like a lump of thick blancmange suspended in fluid in your skull, held in place by nerves, blood vessels and the spinal cord. If you fall at speed or receive a hard blow such as a kick, the effect is to bounce the brain against the sides of the skull or twist it on its attachments.

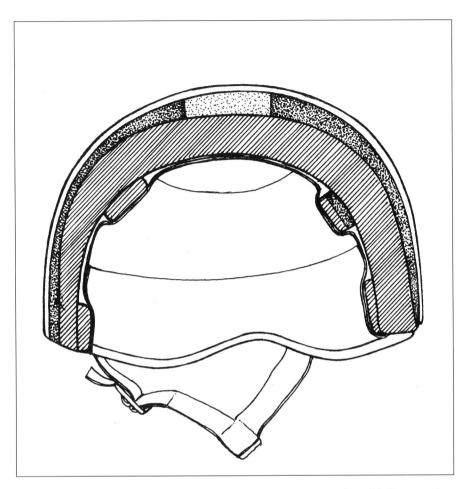

This cross-section of a hat shows the different layers of padded protection beneath the outer shell.

What a hat has to do is try to slow down that impact so that your brain is cushioned and, consequently, suffers less damage. That is why the inside of a riding hat is made of thick, polystyrene-type material, formed of layers of bubbles that burst on impact and gradually diffuse the effect rather than allow the material to be pushed out of shape. This layer is usually the same thickness all round so your head is protected from as many angles as possible. Some older hats such as the BS 4472 had drawlaces inside the crown. These, too, were designed to slow the impact, but only really worked if you fell straight down on the top of your head.

The outer shell is there to stop sharp objects like stones getting through and in 1998, one of the safety tests was modified to simulate a blow from a sharp edge such as a horseshoe. If you wear a hat with a fixed peak, the peak must be constructed to bend or snap on impact.

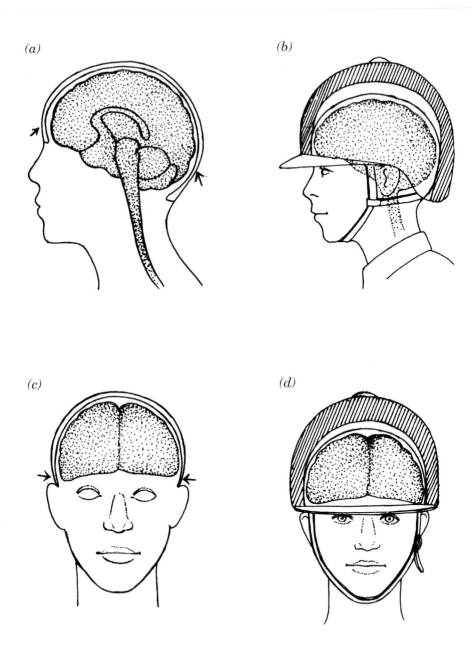

(a)

(b)

(c)

(d)

Arrows indicate where the scull is thin (a and c). The modern riding hat protects the head and in particular the vulnerable areas (b and d).

A hat should cover the areas of the skull shown on the previous page, because they are particularly thin and vulnerable. The forehead and back of the skull are especially important. There has been some controversy over how far down the forehead a hat should cover — for example, jockeys need room for their protective goggles and sometimes found that they had to push the early PAS 015 hats back to accommodate them- while some people argue that a hat which slips forward could break your nose. However, with the PAS 015 98 the 'goggle problem' has been addressed (which should also help riders who wear spectacles); and in the end your nose can be more easily mended than your brain. If your hat fits properly, it should not slip. Always wear it parallel to the ground and never push it further back on your head than it is designed to fit.

a)   *b)*

The hats in these pictures do not fit correctly a) too far back, b) too low over forehead

Whether you wear a show hat with a peak or a jockey skull, recommended standards change from time to time so it is a good idea to keep an eye on what is new so that you know what to look for when buying. When a new hat standard is introduced, you may not have to rush out and buy a new hat immediately but if you are competing or taking part in Pony Club or riding club activities, check the current rules. Most organisations and disciplines now expect a minimum standard to be worn (in Britain this is usually BSEN 1384 or PAS 015) but when the most recent standards were introduced the Pony Club, for example, gave members at least a year to comply with them.

Correct Dress for Riders

In order to become safer, riding hats have had to become bigger, but the modern jockey skull (left) worn with a velvet cover and show hat with a peak (right) can still look smart.

For some competitors a jockey skull must be worn with a silk cover.

A correctly fitted show hat with leather chin harness.

The shape and construction of riding hats has changed quite a lot in recent years. The main problem with safer hats is that when we first see them, we think they are too ugly and ungainly to wear, but they always seem to catch on when we get used to the idea. Something as large as a motorcycle helmet would probably be impractical but, in order to become safer, riding hats have had to became bigger thankfully, riders seem to be getting a little less vain and a lot more sensible. As the pictures on the opposite page and below show, modern hats can still look smart.

An example of a PAS O15 worn with a black lycra hat cover.

There are still some exceptions, such as top level dressage, where top hats are required, and some showing classes, in which top hats or bowlers may be worn, but most disciplines now decree that at competitions a hat to the recommended standard, correctly adjusted and fastened, must be worn at all times when mounted. For competitions, jockey skulls are worn with either a velvet cover or a coloured silk depending on the discipline — again, check the relevant rules.

Ventilation

Some people find hats too hot, especially in the summer, and would like ventilation holes as may be found in some imported hats from countries such as New Zealand and the USA. However, British safety experts believe there is a chance that a sharp object could penetrate the holes so, since our climate isn't as hot as New Zealand or North America, large ventilation holes are not likely to be approved here. Hat manufacturers have tried to get round the heat problem by using different linings to make life more comfortable and less sweaty, so shop around.

Buying a hat

In Britain the current standards are BSEN 1384, EN 1384 and PAS 015; but bear in mind that this could change and always check with your chosen discipline or a BETA retailer. Any hat you buy should conform to at least one of these standards. It should carry the BSI kitemark so that you know it has been safety-tested to the given standard. Never buy a second-hand hat as you have no way of telling whether it has been damaged.

Fitting

Correct fit is vital. Seek advice from a retailer who has been specially trained in hat-fitting by BETA — you will see the certificate displayed in their store. Shop around to find a hat that fits perfectly and is comfortable — different brands may vary slightly in shape and there is no reason to be uncomfortable. When buying for children, do not allow growing room as this will result in the hat not fitting correctly.

Harness

The retention harness is also important. Wear it fastened at all times — however good the hat, it is no use if it falls off before you hit the ground. The harness must be fitted properly but is no substitute for a correctly fitting hat. It should stop the hat from slipping in any direction . The harness must be fixed to the hat at three or four points and although the buckle is often at one side of your face, ideally it should lie under your chin so that it will not damage your jaw bone on impact. Chin cups generally do not allow such a good fit — some people like to brace their jaw against the chin cup, but if you fall, your jaw relaxes so the harness will no longer fit. Also, there is a tendency for chin cups to slide up the face and cause considerable damage there.

Three point harness side view   *Three point harness rear view*

Labels to look for:

The standard — currently EN (or BSEN) 1384 and PAS 015

The BSI kitemark

You should also see a CE mark. This is important, but it is not a standard (like EN or PAS) so is not enough on its own.

When buying a hat look for the kitemark - proof that it has been safely tested to the given standard

The interior of a child's hat note the kitemark, the BSEN number and the letters CE (communauté Européenne).

Correct Dress for Riders

You MUST buy a new hat if:

• you have outgrown your existing one.

• your existing hat has received a hard blow or you were concussed as a result. Although the damage may not be visible, the protection will have been significantly reduced.

Otherwise, it is generally recommended that you change your hat approximately every six years.

From time to time, the British Horse Society conducts accident surveys and may collect damaged hats for information purposes. If you have a hat that might be suitable for this research, telephone the Society on 01926 707700. They will also need details of the accident and the injuries that occurred or, indeed, were averted.

These pictures show cross-sections of hats that have been involved in accidents. The damage could not be seen until the hat was opened.

Body protectors

Anyone who rides at fast speeds or over fixed fences is strongly advised to wear a body protector. The benefits of this important piece of equipment have been well demonstrated in the world of National Hunt racing, where the incidence of cracked ribs (caused by fallen jockeys being kicked) has been dramatically reduced since the wearing of body protectors became compulsory. Body protectors are manufactured in a variety of styles – shop around to find one which suits your figure.

As with hats, standards for body protectors now exist and are recommended at certain levels in high-risk sports outside racing, such as horse trials. In Britain, body protectors manufactured to British Equestrian Trade Association (BETA) standards are recommended.

The current BETA standard, which is a performance standard and meets all the requirements of the European Personal Protective Equipment (PPE) Directive, is available in three classes:

Class 1 - Green Label: Protectors providing a low level of protection that is probably only acceptable in low-risk situations.

Class 2 - Orange Label: Protectors providing a 'normal' level of protection for general use.

Class 3 - Purple Label: Protectors providing enhanced protection for use in higher risk situations and by older riders with more brittle bones or by riders desiring better protection.

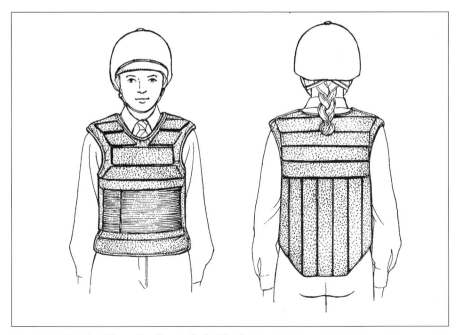

An example of a Class 1 - Green Label body protector.

15

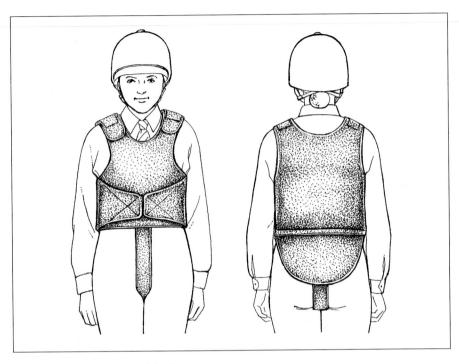

A Class 2 - Orange Label body protector.

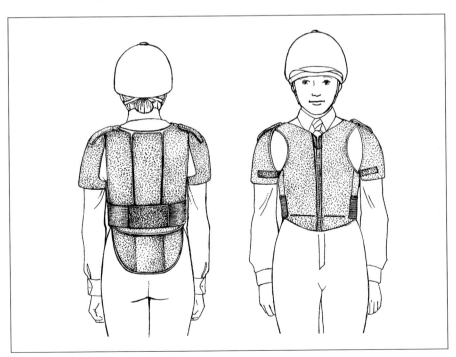

A Class 3 - Purple Label body protector.

Most body protectors come with separate shoulder protectors, though in some garments they are an integral part of the design. Because the shoulder is stronger than the rib cage and a quite different shape, shoulder protectors are given a separate standard.

When choosing a body protector, ensure that it fits well, is comfortable and does not restrict movement. If the shoulder protectors are a separate feature, it may be possible to adjust the garment at the shoulder as well as elsewhere. All body protectors should come with detailed instructions concerning how to fit them and how to take care of them (washing, etc).

The garment should cover the whole circumference of the torso. At the front, the bottom edge should be not less than 25cm (9 3/4″) below the rib cage and should reach the level of the pelvis laterally. The top should reach the top of the sternum or breastbone.

At the back the edge should be not less than 15cm (8″) below the level of the top of the pelvis on the average adult. The top of the garment should reach the level of the seventh cervical vertebrae (the prominent bone at the base of the neck). The armholes should be roughly circular in shape and as small as is comfortable.

Footnote
- To comply with European law, all PPE (personal protective equipment) manufactured after 1 July 1995 has to carry the CE mark. The CE mark does not represent a new standard, it merely shows that the Trading Standards of several countries consider it suitable for the purpose for which it was made. The CE mark should not be confused with the CEN European Standard (still in draft form at the time of writing).

Footwear

The safest footwear for riding is the leather riding boot or jodhpur boot (the latter, preferably, should have elasticated sides as straps and buckles can become caught up). Rubber riding boots and strong lace-up shoes with plain soles and 1.5cm (1/2″) heels are also acceptable although non-leather soles do not give such good protection as leather ones.

Wellington boots, trainers and other footwear with ridged soles or with little or no heel should not be worn. Ridged soles can become caught up in the stirrups, while footwear with no clearly defined heel can slip right through the iron. Both situations are highly dangerous in the event of a fall, since the foot might be trapped in the stirrup and the rider dragged.

(For recommendations and rules on running shoes worn for endurance riding, see *Chapter 7*.)

Above: two examples of footware which should never be used for riding.

Left and above left: leather riding boots with correctly fitted garter straps and spurs. Note the clearly defined heel for maximum safety.

Spectacles, contact lenses and goggles

Although there is undeniably an element of danger in riding in spectacles, many people do so all their lives without suffering injury. Ideally, however, those with defective vision should wear contact lenses, of which the soft type is the most advisable. Under Jockey Club rules, which also cover point-to-pointing, only soft or 'perma' (the type of lens which can be worn for extended periods of time) are permitted and vision-corrected goggles are not allowed (see also *Chapter 11*).

If you are unable to wear contact lenses, then your optician may recommend spectacles with either plastic or metal frames, fitted with toughened glass, plastic, or impact-resistant or polycarbonate lenses (the latter are tougher than plastic but scratch easily). Anther safety factor of some frames is a soft, aluminium bridge. When choosing spectacles which you intend to wear when riding, check with your optician on the latest safety features with regard to shatter-proof lenses, etc.

Racing goggles should also be chosen with care. Polycarbonate are recommended within the industry, since they are flexible, comfortable and optically correct. PVC or plastic can alter the vision, while cheap plastic ones may crack and could injure the eyes. Remember to choose goggles that are non-misting on the inside. For those working in racing stables with all-weather gallops, it is worth mentioning that particles of all-weather surfaces have been known to damage the eye by causing an acute chemical reaction. This could lead to permanent damage or loss of sight, so the wearing of suitable goggles is a sensible precaution.

Jewellery

With the exception of a plain bar tie-pin, jewellery should not be worn when riding. Earrings, however small, are particularly dangerous because they can become caught on trees or in your jacket collar or the chinstrap of your hat and can cause nasty injuries to your ears. Nose-rings are just as dangerous.

● Tie-pins should always be worn horizontally or at an angle. A tie-pin worn vertically could hurt your chest or your chin if it becomes knocked downwards or upwards.

Hair

Long hair should always be tied back or plaited and put up when you are working around horses. If it is not, there is a danger that it might become caught up or frighten a horse if it suddenly flaps in his face. (See page 34)

Road safety aids

Because of the ever-increasing quantity of modern-day traffic and the high speeds at which much of it travels, horses and riders are especially vulnerable when they venture out on to the roads. And if riding on the roads in daylight is dangerous, then riding on the roads in poor light conditions or after dark is doubly so. Unfortunately it is something which cannot always be avoided, but there is no excuse for not making yourself and your horse as conspicuous as possible – and that applies whatever the time of day.

A whole range of clothing for horse and rider is now available in bright, reflective materials designed to make the wearers visible to other road users at long distances, both during the day and at night, and to make them instantly visible in potentially dangerous situations, such as on narrow lanes and on bends.

Future research will no doubt produce new ideas but currently it is Dayglo materials that are found to give the highest visibility, with yellow recommended as the best colour. Being very bright, it is ideal for use in daylight.

To be suitable for after-dark use, Dayglo items should be fitted with strips of 'retro-reflective' material, consisting of millions of little 'beads'. In daylight these strips appear grey but after dark they give brilliant reflection of light.

By wearing clothes in these materials and kitting your horse out in similarly designed tack and boots (the latter are particularly effective because of the movement of the horse's legs) you can ensure that both of you are as conspicuous as possible to other road users.

Horse and rider wearing high visibility road safety equipment.

A Sam Browne belt is a useful alternative to a tabard.

It makes sense to wear the following specially designed high-visibility items of clothing whenever you ride on the road:
- Hat cover: in Dayglo yellow fitted with retro-reflective strip.
- Tabard: in Dayglo yellow fitted with retro-reflective strip, preferably encircling the whole body. Tabards can be inscribed with a warning message, but bear in mind that if there are too many words drivers may approach too close for comfort in order to be able to read them. A large 'L' for learner is a good alternative for novice riders and for riders on young horses.

OR

Body warmer: in Dayglo yellow fitted with retro-reflective strips.

OR

Sam Browne belt: in Dayglo yellow with retro-reflective strips.
- Arm and leg bands: in dayglo yellow fitted with retro-reflective strips.
- Safety lights: can be attached to the rider's boots or tabard.

NB In Britain the law requires that children under the age of 14 must wear an approved safety helmet, securely fastened, when riding on the roads. Although cycling helmets are permitted, the Pony Club strongly recommends the wearing of hats specifically designed for horse riding.

Safety Checklist

- Always wear a hat when mounted, at the correct angle and with the chin-strap correctly adjusted and fastened.
- Whenever possible wear your own hat: a borrowed one is unlikely to give the same protection as one that has been fitted to your particular size and shape of head.
- Always replace a hat that has been subjected to impact. (By sending the hat, plus details of any injury sustained, to the British Horse Society's Safety Department at Stoneleigh for entry into the Head and Spinal Injuries' Database, you can help the Society with its valuable research into riding accidents.)
- Never ride in Wellington boots, trainers or shoes with ridged soles, or footwear without heels 1.5cm (1/2") deep.
- Never ride in boots which have been repaired with half-soles - which, should you have a fall, could catch your foot in the stirrup (particularly if the sole has worn loose.)
- Always use the correct stirrup size - about one inch wider than your boot - and check that the stirrup leathers will slide easily off the stirrup bar: this is vital if you fall and are in danger of being dragged.
- Always wear fluorescent/reflective garments when riding on the road and fit your horse with fluorescent/reflective leg bands.
- Check your tack regularly, particularly the stitching, for signs of wear.
- Never ride in leather gloves in wet weather - the reins will slip through them.

2
Clothes for the Job

There is a tendency among non-horsey people to crack jokes about riding clothes, as if they were some strange kind of fancy dress, sported by riders simply to show off. Nothing, of course, could be further from the truth: virtually all items of modern riding gear are designed for comfort, ease of movement, and safety – the most obvious exceptions being one or two styles of traditional headwear, such as the top hat.

Riding is an athletic pastime. When the horse is on the move the rider's body is constantly moving, too. The faster the paces and the more jumping, the more energetic the rider's movements. Clothes must therefore be designed to 'give' with those movements if they are to be comfortable and not restrict the rider or simply come apart at the seams.

Nowadays there is a bewildering range of suitable clothing available to the rider. The range is constantly changing and growing as new materials come on to the market; and people's needs alter because of developments in their sports. There are clothes to suit all pockets and although the more expensive products will as a general rule last longer, there are plenty of budget-priced items that will do the job perfectly well.

One word of warning: it should be borne in mind that, useful though they undoubtedly are, some modern, man-made fabrics (particularly waterproofs) are very noisy – creaking and crackling with every movement. At best they can be distracting to a horse, at worst, particularly on a windy day, they can cause serious problems with an animal which is spooky.

Hats

The most essential item of equipment for all riders, and one on which there should be no economy, is a hard hat. If you fall off, it is a long way to the ground, particularly when jumping. Under Pony Club rules and the rules of most equestrian sports a hard hat must be worn at all times when mounted. Full details of current hat specifications and correct fitting are included in Chapter 1, and details of *specific* requirements for each sport are given in the appropriate chapter.

Footwear

Riding boots are designed to provide comfort – by protecting the shin bone – ease of movement and, most important, safety. There is no more potentially lethal situation than to fall off and have a foot caught in the stirrup-iron. Therefore, with all footwear for riding it is important for the soles to be smooth, so that they will slide easily out of the stirrup-iron in an emergency. The heels must be a minimum of 1.5cm ($1/2''$) deep to prevent the foot slipping right through the iron. Note that deep treads on the soles of boots will not slip free of the stirrup – particularly if it has a rubber tread.

Jodhpur boots

As their name implies, jodhpur boots are ideal for wearing with jodhpurs. The elastic-sided ones are best; those which fasten with a strap are more likely to become caught up, particularly during an activity as energetic as mounted games, when riders have to jump on and off their ponies a great many times. Some riders prefer elastic-sided jodhpur boots to riding boots because they allow maximum flexibility of the ankle.

Left: For everyday use, rubber riding boots are a safe, practical alternative to leather ones.

Below Left: Jodphur boots with elastic sides are safer than those which are fastened with straps.

Below: Paddock boots are safe to ride in, and they look smart, especially when worn with half-chaps.

Riding boots

Riding boots should be close-fitting to the leg, for comfort, neatness and to keep water out. They should cover the length of the calf but should not impede the knee-joint when fully bent. The best ones are made of leather, although rubber ones are a suitable alternative for everyday wear. Newmarket boots, which have canvas tops, and field boots, which have laces at the ankle, are also suitable.

The leg should fit as closely as possible, but remember that in winter you may want to wear thick tights under your breeches and, especially with rubber boots, to insert an inner sole or to wear a thermal sock for added warmth.

Garter straps

Garter straps, if used, should be worn with the buckle towards the front of the knee against the seam of the breeches, with the free end of the strap pointing outwards. If the straps are too long, they should be trimmed 1.5cm (1/2″) beyond the last keeper.

Shoes

Strong lace-up walking shoes are acceptable in place of jodhpur or riding boots, as long as they have smooth soles and a medium heel.

Legwear

Close-fitting legwear has long been an essential part of the rider's wardrobe. It protects the skin from being chafed through constant contact with the saddle and stirrup leathers. Those who try to ride in loose-fitting trousers usually find that in time their legs become pinched and sore.

Jodhpurs and breeches are the traditional items of legwear for riders, though nowadays there is also a wide range of specially designed riding trousers on the market, often economically priced and therefore especially suitable for everyday use around the stables, for hacking out, and so on. All three types of legwear must be reinforced where the leg lies on the saddle with strappings, either in the same material as the garment or in suede or suede-look material. The last two make the garment more expensive but give the best protection. An inset seat-panel made in special extra-grip fabric will also increase both comfort and security in the saddle.

Breeches, jodhpurs and riding trousers come in all sorts of fabrics. The material ranges from thermal with brushed cotton backing (for maximum warmth and comfort in the coldest winter weather), wool cord, ribbed wool, corduroy, heavyweight cotton with Lycra, needlecord or nylon, to lightweight cotton suitable for riding in hot weather. Many materials include some degree of stretch, since it ensures a better fit and enables the garment to 'give' with the rider's movements (remember, though, that very close-fitting multi-stretch garments are not very attractive on the larger human figure).

The choice of material will be governed partly by individual preference, partly by cost, and partly by weather conditions and type of riding. Nylon jodhpurs, for instance, are relatively cheap but will not keep out the cold. Good quality cotton ones, while costing more, are cool in summer yet warm in winter.

As with riding boots, remember that in winter you may wish to wear long underwear for extra warmth, in which case you must allow extra room under breeches or jodhpurs.

All types of modern legwear come in a wide range of colours. Dark tones are especially useful for everyday wear since they do not show the dirt so much and require less washing. But traditional light-coloured jodhpurs and breeches (usually fawn) are essential for most competitive riding.

Also available for casual wear are hard-wearing chaps, made of hide or suede, and designed to be pulled on over jeans or trousers and fastened to a belt at the waist; and knee-length gaiter chaps (half chaps) or leggings, which are fitted with straps under the knee, zips or Velcro down the sides and elastic under the foot, and are suitable for wear with breeches and jodhpur boots.

Chaps are designed to be worn over trousers or jeans and are useful for leisure riding. The full-length chaps in this photograph are made of washable material.

25

Jackets

Riding jacket

A well-made, lined riding jacket gives protection against the weather, when you are riding through woods, etc, and also in the event of a fall. It should be made of a serviceable brownish or greeny-grey tweed (known as Derby or Keeper's tweed) or covert cloth in a style specially designed for riding. It should have one or two vents at the back and should be free from adornments such as velvet collar (except in the show ring), fancy buttons or brightly coloured lining. Remember when fitting a jacket that it must allow free movement of the arms and shoulders, particularly when jumping.

Hunting coat

The same principles apply to hunting coats as to riding jackets. The heavier the cloth, the better the protection. Hunting coats come in different colours – black, blue, green and red being the most usual. For details see sections on hunting, horse trials, showing and show jumping.

Casual coats

There is no shortage of good casual coats – anoraks, quilted jackets, body warmers, blousons and so on – specially designed for everyday riding. However, such casual wear is not suitable for lessons or for Pony Club rallies, because bulky, rather shapeless garments make it difficult for an instructor to assess a rider's position. Casual coats are not acceptable for competitions or hunting, either.

Shirts

A plain shirt with a well-fitting collar is correct with an ordinary tie. With a hunting tie (or 'stock') a shirt without a collar but with a well-fitting neck-band is most suitable. In show jumping, American-type women's riding shirts (with a high collar) are also permitted. They enable the wearer to dispense with a tie altogether. Some have a detachable collar and so can be worn with a hunting tie when required. For details of colour requirements for shirts, see the rules of individual sports.

Neckwear

Ties

Generally speaking, the correct wear with a riding jacket is a conventional tie, fastened with a plain bar tie-pin. But for showing, hunting and other disciplines, check the relevant sections of this book, as there are occasional variations (for example, in show jumping a white tie may

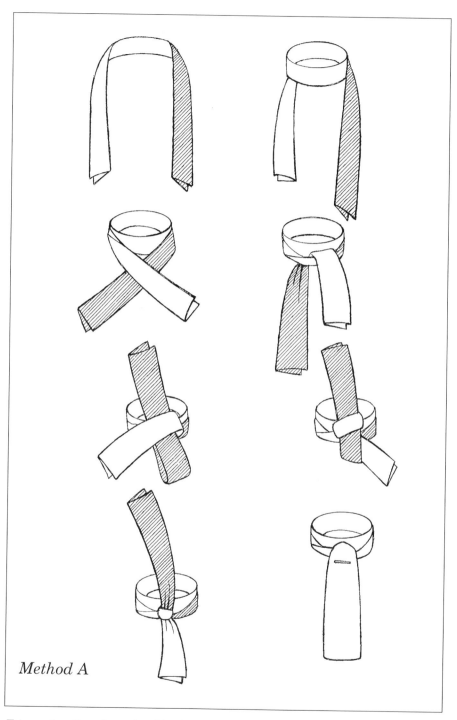

Method A

Tying a hunting tie, or 'stock'. There are two correct methods, illustrated in the line drawings.

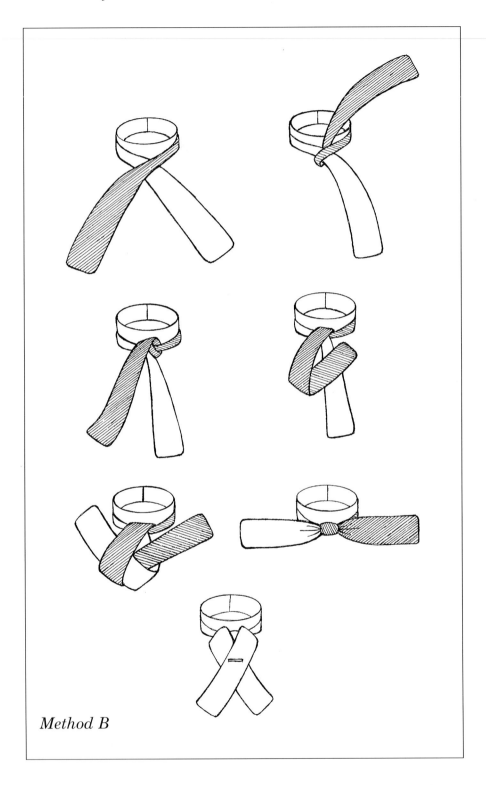

Method B

be worn instead of a hunting tie, with a blue, black, red or green jacket).

Pony Club members may wear a Pony Club tie and plain bar tie-pin. After the age of about fifteen it is acceptable to wear a hunting tie (stock) with a tweed coat. The tie should be white or in a dark, spotted material.

With a hunting coat it is usual to wear a white hunting tie and a plain bar tie-pin.

Tying a hunting tie, or 'stock':
The photographs show an abbreviated
version of Method B.

General notes on hunting ties

- If the tie is a shaped one, be sure to choose the correct neck-size, otherwise it will not fit correctly.
- The tie must be firmly, correctly and neatly tied (see diagrams).
- Hunting ties are not suitable for very young riders, as their necks are not long enough so the ties do not fit.
- Hunting ties have been known to save lives, as they give protection in bad falls and could even prevent a broken neck. They can also be used as bandages to control bleeding.

Gloves

Gloves should be worn for most competitions (see the rules for individual sports), for shows, and for hunting. They give protection against the cold and rain and provide a better grip when reins are sweaty or rain soaked.

Always buy gloves that are specially designed for riding. They come in a variety of materials and styles (including fingerless ones) and may have such features as pimple palm grips or other 'extra-grip' properties, reinforced rein fingers, elasticated or Velcro wrist fastenings and Lycra inserts for added flexibility.

The choice of glove depends very much on the use to which it will be put. For dressage schooling, for example, leather gloves are preferable as they ensure a much truer 'feel', but bear in mind that they are not suitable for use in wet weather as the reins will tend to slip through them. For other purposes, gloves may be made of cotton, string or nylon and may be lined or unlined. For everyday riding, choose gloves that wash well. Always wear gloves (preferably leather) when lungeing. If you are going to spend a long time in the saddle on a wet day, carry a spare pair tucked beneath the girth under the saddle flap.

Underwear

Specially designed sports underwear can be far more comfortable than conventional garments, and many riding-wear companies also stock a range of suitable underwear for both men and women.

Underbreeches are particularly useful in cold weather. Designed to go under breeches or jodhpurs, they are fitted with a stirrup foot to prevent ride-up and have no uncomfortable gusset or inside-leg seams. They are made in a variety of materials, including thermal. For women there are sport tops featuring non-slip shoulder straps, deep arm holes for maximum freedom of movement, and a deep body to prevent ride-up and excess 'bounce'. There are also various designs of briefs, for both sexes, some of which include a padded seat – a great comfort for skinny people!

Waterproofs

Modern waterproofing techniques have made wet-weather wear lighter and more comfortable than the old-style double-texture mackintoshes, which looked smart but were rather bulky. Nowadays waxed cotton is a great favourite and there are various 'breathable' waterproof fabrics which are very comfortable to wear, though they do tend to be expensive. Nylon waterproofs are far cheaper, but are less comfortable and afford little warmth.

Waterproof coats may be short, three-quarter or full length. A long coat should be fitted with a rear vent and leg straps; shorter ones need side vents for riding comfort. Many coats feature a cotton or fleece lining and corduroy collar for additional comfort and warmth. A storm collar, storm cuffs and pommel flap are other useful fittings, and for riding for long periods in wet weather (for example, out hunting) a mackintosh apron gives added protection. It should come down to just below the join between the boot and the breeches.

Remember that some horses, as mentioned earlier, object to flapping waterproofs. If you have a spooky horse, choose a 'quiet' material and a short coat. Wax chaps can be worn to keep your legs dry.

For maximum safety, waterproof clothing should fit well and be made of a 'quiet', non-crackly material.

31

General turnout

A good rider takes pride in his own appearance as well as that of his horse. A neat, clean and correct turnout is a pleasing sight. It also makes practical sense because it encourages safe and effective riding.

Care of riding clothes

All riding clothes should be kept clean: jackets need regular brushing; breeches, jodhpurs and shirts regular washing; and boots regular polishing.

Jackets

Jackets should always be kept on hangers. Before wearing your jacket make sure that all the buttons are secure.

Mud should be removed from tweed coats with a stiff brush. Never brush coats when they are wet, as mud smears.

Superficial mud on red, blue or black coats may be scraped off with a knife. The coat, when dry, may then be brushed. Otherwise a muddy coat should be washed down as soon as possible after use with a stiff brush and plenty of water (soft rainwater is traditionally considered best) and hung to dry well away from any direct source of heat. When dry, the coat may be brushed. If the collar is made of velvet, it should be pinned down to prevent shrinkage as the coat dries. If you are not going to wear your coat for any length of time, take the opportunity to send it to the cleaners.

Breeches and jodhpurs

Wool cord and cavalry twill breeches should be soaked in a mild detergent and gently scrubbed the following day. For breeches and jodhpurs made of other materials follow the washing instructions – most can be put in the washing machine.

Boots

Always use trees to keep your boots in good shape. When you have eased the tree into the boot, turn the boot upside down and push it over the tree to prevent wrinkling and to make polishing easier. If you have no boot trees, stuff your boots firmly with newspaper.

Use a blunt knife to remove mud (a small, stiff brush and warm water should be used to remove mud from the welts and soles). Give the boots a good spongeing over, being careful to remove all the sweat from the insides, then wipe with a dry cloth and leave to dry. Never put boots near direct heat: it will ruin the leather. When dry, work in with a brush a good quality boot polish. A little dubbin brushed into the creases at the ankle will help to keep the leather soft.

The traditional way to prepare hunting boots (made of reversed hide) is to 'bone' them. Polish is first applied to the boots with a cloth and then boned in with the shank bone of a deer, which has a very smooth surface. A warm spoon or the bone handle of a knife may be used if there is no deer-shank bone to hand. Leaving the polish on the boots overnight before boning begins is said to give the best finish. Rubbing the bone over the surface of the polish gives the leather a distinctive finish.

Rubber boots should also be polished after washing; a liquid polish is the most suitable.

Never leave boots lying about on the floor. Stand them on their own two feet.

Hats

Hats should be hung up when not in use. Never leave a wet hunting cap resting on its brim for long, as this will warp it. Stuff it with crumpled newspaper to keep it raised, or use a wine bottle which makes an excellent hat stand.

Crash-hat covers should be washed according to the washing instructions.

Bowler hats should be allowed to dry before being brushed clean. Velvet caps may be held over steaming water and sponged clean without causing damage to the velvet. Otherwise they should be allowed to dry and then brushed clean, but not with too hard a brush as this will damage the velvet. Top hats should be cleaned by spongeing off the dirt with water, or brushing – again not with too hard a brush.

Hair

The effect of neat, well-fitting clothes can be ruined if a rider's hair is untidy. Nothing looks worse than a riding hat crammed on top of an unruly mop of hair.

Men and boys look best if their hair is not too long at the back, and there should be no stray strands hanging down over the eyes. Women and girls with anything other than a short style should wear their hair in a net. The following points will ensure a neat appearance:

- Hair worn in a net should be kept well away from your collar, otherwise it will flop up and down, giving an impression of untidy riding and showing up any defects in your balance and rhythm.
- Longish hair should be put up into a bun. If you must wear a pony tail, tie it with a plain, dark band.
- Never wear fancy ribbons or brightly coloured slides.
- Very long hair should be plaited and secured with a dark elastic band. For girls up to the age of twelve or thirteen the plait looks more suit able worn free. For older girls and women it should be twisted into a neat bun.

Long hair should be plaited, secured with a dark elastic band, twisted into a bun, and covered with a hairnet.

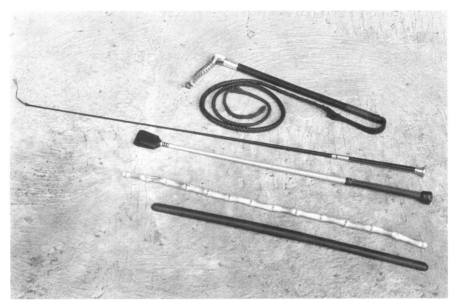

Types of whip. From top: hunting whip with thong and lash; dressage whip; cutting whip; plain cane; leather-covered cane.

Whips

All whips should be sponged clean after use. The thong of a hunting whip will need scrubbing clean with a brush and warm water. When dry, it should be treated with saddle soap to keep it soft.

Spurs

Spurs should have blunt ends, bending downwards. The straps should be the same colour as the boot. The spur should lie along the seam of the boot above the heel, with the longer part on the outside, the buckle close to the spur, and the loose end trimmed to 2.5cm (1″) beyond the buckle.

3
On The Ground

Horses and ponies are big, strong animals who require skilful training and careful handling. Even then they can be unpredictable and given to making sudden movements which, on occasion, can take the most experienced of horsemen by surprise. It is important, therefore, to wear sensible clothes when working with horses on the ground as well as when riding – clothing that affords complete freedom of movement coupled with a degree of protection. The ability to move out of the way quickly has saved many a handler from being leaned on, bitten, trodden on, kicked or otherwise hurt by an unexpected lapse of good manners on the part of their equine friend.

Clothes for stable work

Neat, well-fitting (but not too tight) clothing is easier to move around in than loose, flapping garments, which can so easily become caught up on 'foreign objects', such as the bolt of a door or the handle of a wheel barrow.

Depending on the weather, a shirt, sweatshirt or sweater is ideal for work around the stables. If it is cold enough to wear a body warmer or jacket, you should keep it fastened: a flapping coat can easily become caught up and it might even frighten or distract a nervous horse. It also looks untidy and unworkmanlike. The same applies to flapping hair.

In very hot weather there is always the temptation to wear flimsy, sleeveless T-shirts or suntops. Be warned! If a horse unexpectedly swings his head round to bite – and he may well do so if he is being irritated by flies or is simply ticklish when being groomed – his teeth can make very painful contact with a bare upper arm or shoulder. If, on the other hand, you are wearing a shirt with sleeves, even short ones, there is at least a chance that the teeth will grab the material, not your skin!

Comfortable jeans, trousers or jodhpurs (dark coloured ones are the most practical) are all suitable for stable work. Again, they should fit well, without being so tight that they make bending down difficult.

Clothes for stable work should be neat and comfortable.

Footwear

No one has yet invented the perfect all-round footwear for working with horses on the ground. When mucking out, particularly in wet weather, there is probably nothing to beat the good old-fashioned 'wellie' boot - it is waterproof, easily washed clean and the soles give plenty of grip under most conditions. On the minus side, wellington boots tend to make your feet cold, though this problem can be largely overcome by choosing a boot half a size bigger than your feet and wearing good walking-boot, or other thick, socks. Wellingtons can, however, be rather cumbersome at the best of times and you could find yourself less nimble on your feet than you might like. Nor do they afford a great deal of protection against an iron-shod hoof, should one descend on your foot.

The same can be said of the ubiquitous 'trainers', which so many people find the most comfortable of modern casual footwear. However, they do at least enable you to move quickly when the necessity arises and if they are made of stout material they will afford some protection should a horse tread on you.

Jodhpur boots and leather riding boots probably give as good protection to the feet as anything. Though you may not wish to make them dirty when mucking out or grooming, they are certainly ideal (and look smart) for activities such as lungeing or long-reining.

A recent addition to some riding and jodhpur boots is the steel toecap, designed to protect your foot if a horse does happen to step on it. Opinion differs as to the benefits of such reinforcements. A human foot may well be protected by such a device from a lightly placed equine hoof, but if a horse really puts his weight down, won't he simply crush the toecap into your foot?

Always fasten your jacket when working around horses.

Correct dress for lungeing.

Lungeing and long-reining

Always wear gloves when lungeing or long-reining a horse. They give extra grip on the rein(s) and prevent rope-burns should the horse suddenly pull away. Remember: never coil the lunge-rein around your hand; if the horse pulls away, your hand could become caught. Always wear a hard hat, with the chin-strap correctly fastened.

Leading a horse

Many horses are led about with no thought of the handler's safety – with one hand on a headcollar, or gripping a piece of string, perhaps; or by someone wearing clothes which afford little protection or in which they could not possibly move quickly should the need arise. It has to be said that in most cases horses behave perfectly well and no harm is done. But accidents can happen even with the calmest animal. If there is any possibility of a led horse being frightened by something unfamiliar – or if you are simply unfamiliar with him and don't know how he behaves when being led – then take sensible precautions: wear a hard hat, just in case he rears up and strikes out. Wear gloves. And wear boots to protect your feet should he jump about. He should of course be led on a suitable lead-rein or rope which will give you some degree of control should he play up. Young horses are particularly unpredictable, so be prepared.

Instructors

Riding instructors should always be correctly dressed in riding gear, including hard hat, breeches or jodhpurs, and boots. Like everyone else working with horses on the ground, they may need to move quickly to get out of the way of a loose horse or to protect themselves from a flying hoof. They may well need to climb aboard a pupil's horse to demonstrate a point – quite apart from which, being correctly dressed sets the right example.

Safety Checklist

- Always wear a hard hat and gloves when lungeing or long-reining, and also when leading a young horse or one with whom you are not familiar.
- Always wear comfortable, well-fitting clothes and footwear that allow you complete freedom of movement.
- Never wear sandals or other flimsy shoes when working with horses.
- Do not wear T-shirts and sun tops.
- Do not wear baggy, flapping garments.
- Do not wear jewellery.

4
Leisure Riding

While all organised equestrian sports have their own rules governing participants' dress, the individual rider is, of course, free to wear whatever he or she chooses when taking part in non-competitive activities such as schooling, hacking out and so on. When riding on the roads, with all the potential dangers that it involves, the only legal requirement concerns children under the age of fourteen, who must wear an approved safety helmet.

The onus is therefore on the individual to behave in a responsible manner when deciding what to wear for everyday riding. By taking sensible precautions you will not only guard against injury but you could also save other people a good deal of trouble.

Whether you are schooling, doing road work or perhaps enjoying a trekking holiday, as always there are two golden rules governing the rider's equipment: it must be safe, to protect you from injury, and it should be comfortable, to enable you to perform to your best ability.

Schooling at home and off-road hacking

Sweaters, sweatshirts, casual riding coats, trousers and chaps are fine provided you also wear safe footwear and a correctly fitted hat with the harness fastened at all times when you are mounted. (See also *Chapter 1*).

When schooling over cross-country fences it is sensible to take the same precautions that you would when competing: i.e. wear a body protector (see *Chapter 1*).

Riding on the roads

See *Chapter 1* for detailed recommendations regarding safety equipment for both you and your horse.

Riding at a school

No riding establishment worth attending will allow anyone to ride

Suitable leisure riding wear for adults.

Children of varying ages correctly dressed for leisure riding. Note the three different types of footwear.

without a correctly fitted hat and safe footwear. Some schools keep a supply of hats of various sizes which may be borrowed by beginners who do not already have their own. However, a borrowed hat will never fit as well as one fitted to your particular head by a trained person and if you intend to ride regularly, you should buy your own as soon as possible.

When booking a lesson at a school for the first time, check on any dress requirements; it is courteous to be neatly turned out. Remember that if you do wear casual clothes, baggy garments will make it difficult for the instructor to assess your position.

Riding holidays

When booking a non-instructional riding holiday (trekking, post-trekking, day rides, etc) ask the centre's advice regarding appropriate dress and any special items of equipment that you may need.

Everyday Riding Do's and Don'ts

DO:

Wear a correctly fitted hat, with the harness fastened, at all times when you are mounted.

Wear safe footwear at all times, both when you are mounted and when you are moving around horses and ponies.

Wear a body protector if you plan to jump cross-country fences – particularly when schooling a young horse.

Wear comfortable, well-fitting clothes specially designed for riding. If you are uncomfortable, you won't ride to the best of your ability; nor will you be able to concentrate one hundred per cent on what you are doing.

DO NOT:

Wear jewellery. Earrings, necklaces and rings can all become caught up and cause painful injuries, such as ripped ears and even torn-off fingers.

Leave long hair flapping loose. It, too, can easily become caught up and can distract or scare a horse.

Wear your coat unfastened. It looks slovenly, and a flapping coat can distract or scare a horse.

Ride on the road without suitable high-visibility clothing.

5
Pony Club Activities

The rules of the Pony Club require all members to be neatly turned out at all times and to wear correct protective clothing whenever they are mounted. New clothing is not expected, but what is worn should be clean and tidy.

Protective headgear, made to the recommended standard, correctly fitted and worn with the chin-strap fastened, is compulsory for all Pony Club activities, competitive or otherwise. (Note that this ruling on hats applies to all mounted prize-giving ceremonies.) Expert advice should always be sought to ensure that the hat fits correctly. See *Chapter 1*

Jodhpur boots or long riding boots are also compulsory. Trainers, wellingtons and other similar footwear are not permitted for riding. Jeans are not recommended because they can cause chafing. Half-chaps and gaiters may be worn at rallies and in some competitions. They should match the colour of the rider's boots and be of a plain design (no tassles). The wearing of earrings and nose studs is not permitted and may incur elimination from competitions.

At competitive events, while walking the course or when dismounted in the collected ring, riders must be tidily dressed, though not necesarily in riding clothes.

Boys and Girls

Working rallies

PAS 015, BSEN 1384 or BS 4472 crash hat with dark blue or black cover.
Riding jacket.
Shirt with collar and tie.
Sweater or v-necked pullover, without jacket if weather permits.
Jodhpurs or breeches.
Jodhpur boots or riding boots.

- The above is also the correct dress for Associates when instructing. Associates and instructors should at all times be correctly dressed, setting a good example to the children they are teaching.

*Your clothes do not have to be **new** to look good, but they should be **safe** and comfortable. The photographs show a rider and pony **(top)** badly turned out and extremely unsafe, and **(bottom)** correctly turned out.*

Half-chaps with jodhpur boots of matching colour.

- The granting of permission to individual members to wear half-chaps at rallies and team competitions is left to the discretion of the District Commissioners or their appointed chief instructors. The same applies to spurs (which if worn must be blunt, without rowels or sharp edges. If curved, the curve must be downwards and the shank must point straight to the back.)

Mounted Games

PAS 015 or BSEN 1384 crash hat with dark blue or black cover.
White shirt with long sleeves, which should not be rolled up.
White sweatshirt and/or colourless transparent or white waterproof garment with long sleeves may be worn over the shirt in cold or wet weather.
Bib with branch or team colours as appropriate.
Pony Club tie with plain bar tie-pin.
Jodhpurs (fawn or cream).
Jodhpur boots or long boots.

- Jewellery and watches are not allowed.
- Whips and spurs are not allowed.
- The reserve rider, when taking part unmounted, must also wear a hat.
- Badges are optional. If worn, they should be of cloth, not metal, and may be sewn on to the bib.

Correct Dress for Riders

Pony Club members correctly dressed for mounted games, wearing their team tabards.

Note that it easier to run in jodhpur boots than in long riding riding boots.

Dressage

PAS 015 or BSEN 1384 crash hat with dark blue or black cover.
Tweed or dark blue or black coat.
White shirt with collar, and Pony Club tie with plain bar tie-pin

OR

Collarless shirt and white or cream hunting tie with plain bar tie-pin (worn with dark coat); or dark, spotted hunting tie (worn with tweed coat).
Jodhpurs (fawn) with jodhpur boots

OR

Breeches (fawn) with black riding boots.
Gloves.
A whip (of any length) may be carried.
Spurs may be worn if they are made of metal and are blunt, without rowels and have no sharp edges. If curved, the curve must be downwards. The shank must point straight to the back and be not more than 3cm(1¼″) long.
Flowers (in the buttonhole) should not be worn.

Show Jumping

PAS 015 or BSEN 1384 crash hat with dark blue or black cover.
Tweed or dark blue or black coat.
Shirt with collar, and Pony Club tie with plain bar tie-pin (worn with tweed coat)

OR

Collarless shirt with white hunting tie (worn with dark coat); or dark hunting tie (worn with tweed coat).
Jodhpurs (fawn) with jodhpur boots

OR

Breeches (fawn or white) with riding boots.
Gloves (optional).
A whip not less than 45.7 cm (18″) in length and not exceeding 76.2cm (30″) may be carried.
Spurs may be worn. (For details see dressage section, above.)

Horse Trials

Dressage

PAS 015, BSEN 1384 or BS 4472 crash hat with dark blue or black cover.
Tweed or dark blue or black coat.
Shirt with collar, and Pony Club tie with plain bar tie-pin

OR

Correct Dress for Riders

A member in clothes suitable for working rallies and other Pony Club activities such as show jumping and dressage.

Collarless shirt with white or cream hunting tie (worn with dark coat); or dark, spotted hunting tie (worn with tweed coat). Jodhpurs (fawn) with jodhpur boots

OR

Breeches (fawn) with riding boots.
Gloves.
A whip (of any length) may be carried.
Spurs may be worn. (For details see dressage section, above.)

Cross-Country

PAS 015 or BSEN 1384 crash hat with cover in colour of your own choice.
Body protector.
Polo-necked sweater, or long-sleeved shirt with hunting tie.
Jodhpurs (fawn) with jodhpur boots

OR

Breeches (fawn) with riding boots.
Gloves (optional).
A whip not exceeding 76.2cm (30″) in length overall may be carried.
Spurs may be worn. (For details see dressage section, above.)

Correct dress for riding across country in Pony Club competitions.

Show Jumping

PAS 015 or BSEN 1384 crash hat with dark blue or black cover.
Tweed or dark blue or black coat.
Body protector.
Shirt with collar, and Pony Club tie with plain bar tie-pin

OR

Collarless shirt with white or cream hunting tie (worn with dark coat); or dark, spotted hunting tie (worn with tweed coat).
Jodhpurs (fawn) and jodhpur boots

OR

Breeches (fawn) with riding boots.
Gloves (optional).
A whip not exceeding 76.2cm (30″) in length overall may be carried.
Spurs may be worn. (For details see dressage section, above.)

Tetrathlon (riding phase)

As for horse trials cross-country phase.

Polo

PAS 015, BSEN 1384 crash hat or polo helmet. (A polo helmet is compulsory in the Gannon Tournaments.)
Shirt, with number to indicate position of player.
Jodhpurs with jodhpur boots

OR

Breeches/trousers with riding boots.
A whip not exceeding 122cm (48″) in length overall may be carried.
Spurs may be worn provided they do not exceed 3cm in length.
If curved, the curve must be downwards and the shank must point straight to the back.

Polocrosse

PAS 015 or BSEN 1384 crash hat.
Shirt with number, or shirt with numbered tabard, to indicate position of play. Teams should wear matching colours and tabards.
Jodhpurs (fawn) with jodhpur boots

OR

Breeches (fawn) with riding boots.
Knee-pads (brown, black, cream or white) are permitted.
A whip not exceeding 76.2cm (30″) with a flap not less than 5cm (2″) long and 2.5cm (1″) wide may be carried.
Spurs (of the same specification as for dressage, above) may only be used with the written permission of the DistrictCommissioner.
Jewellery and watches are not allowed.
No player may wear buckles or studs on the upper part of his boots or knee-pads in such a way as could damage another player's boots or breeches.

Hunting

PAS 015 or BSEN 1384 crash hat with dark blue or black cover.
Tweed jacket.
Shirt with collar, and Pony Club tie with plain bar tie-pin

OR

Collarless shirt with white or dark, spotted hunting tie (the latter is not suitable for very young members).
Jodhpurs (fawn) with jodhpur boots

OR

Breeches (fawn) with riding boots.
Gloves.
Hunting whip with thong and lash or cutting whip with hunting-whip handle but no thong.
Spurs, if necessary.
Body protector (optional) may be worn under a jacket.

- The list on the previous page is correct dress until you have been given a hunt button, in which case you should wear a red, black or dark blue hunting coat. (See *Chapter 9* for adult hunting dress.)
- Always wear your badge so that the hunt secretary can recognise you as a member of the Pony Club.

Hunter Trials

Although there is no governing body for the sport of hunter trials, and so no universally binding rules regarding dress, there is a tradition for riders in hunter trials to wear 'ratcatcher', or tweed coat, collarless shirt and hunting tie, breeches and hunting boots. (Jodhpurs and jodhpur boots are acceptable for children.)

However, the advent of body protectors, which many people find more comfortable worn over a shirt or sweater than with a jacket, has led to more and more riders wearing cross-country clothes. Most events now accept either mode of dress. Crash hats, with correctly fastened chin-straps, are virtually compulsory.

For Pony Club members competing in hunter trials, the following dress is recommended:

PAS 015 or BSEN 1384 crash hat with dark blue or black cover.
Tweed coat.
Body protector.
Shirt with collar, and tie with plain bar tie-pin

OR

Collarless shirt with hunting tie.
Jodhpurs (fawn) with jodhpur boots

OR

Breeches (fawn) with riding boots.
Gloves.
Spurs, if required. (They must be blunt).

OR

PAS 015 or BSEN 1384 crash hat with cover in colour of your choice.
Long-sleeved shirt or sweater with hunting tie.
Body protector.
Jodhpurs (fawn) with jodhpur boots

OR

Breeches (fawn) with riding boots.
Gloves.
Spurs, if required. (They must be blunt.)

Correct Dress for Riders

A Pony Club junior member corectly dressed for hunting.

An associate member correctly dressed for hunting.

Correct dress for polocrosse.

- It is wise to check in advance any specific dress requirements laid down by the individual hunter trial organisers.

General

- A competitor whose hat comes off or whose chin-strap comes undone in any Pony Club competition must, on penalty of elimination, replace the hat or re-fasten the chin-strap before continuing.

- In dressage the rider may dismount without penalty to recover the hat, or have it passed up from the ground, or may stop without penalty to do up the chin-strap. The same rule applies in show jumping and when riding the cross-country phase of horse trials and in the riding phase of the tetrathlon; in such instances the clock is not stopped. If your hat comes off or your chin-strap comes undone in the middle of a double, treble or multiple obstacle, or at two separate obstacles which are so close together that in the opinion of the fence judge to halt would incur a refusal, you are allowed to negotiate the obstacle(s) first. Any circles which a competitor completes in the course of recovering the hat, or while re-fastening the chin-strap, shall not be penalised as refusals.

- Membership badges should be worn at branch rallies, when hunting, at shows, and at inter-branch competitions. Badges should be kept polished. A coloured disc denoting the wearer's test standard is issued to members by branches. It is worn beneath the membership badge.

6
Dressage

Neatness of turnout is vital in dressage in order to create a harmonious overall appearance of horse and rider. Your boots should be well polished and your clothes spotlessly clean. You can help keep them that way by not putting on your competition jacket until the last moment; and a pair of loose trousers worn over your breeches will help keep the latter clean while unloading, warming up and so on. Keep a clothes brush to hand (and if possible a friend to wield it!) for use just before you go into the arena.

Brightly-coloured clothing, glittering jewellery and eye-catching hair ribbons and buttonholes are definitely out of place. Women with long hair should be particularly careful to ensure that it is worn in such a way (either in a net or plaited up) so as not to attract attention by bouncing about when they are riding.

The top hat worn at the higher levels of dressage competition differs from the traditional hunting top hat, in that the crown is shallower.

For competitions under British Dressage rules the following is correct wear:

Preliminary to Advanced Medium

Crash hat with black, dark blue or brown cover; hunting cap or bowler hat.
Tweed coat. Collarless shirt, dark-coloured hunting tie, and plain bar tie-pin; or shirt with collar, tie, and plain bar tie-pin

OR

Black or dark blue coat and collarless shirt with white or cream hunting tie, and plain bar tie-pin.
White, cream or beige breeches or jodhpurs.
Black or brown riding boots or jodhpur boots.
Gloves.
Spurs.
Whip.

Advanced

Top hat.
Tail coat.
Collarless shirt with white or cream hunting tie.
White, cream or beige breeches.
Black boots.
Gloves.
Spurs.
Whip.

OR

Crash hat, hunting cap or bowler hat.
Black or dark blue coat.
Collarless shirt with white or cream hunting tie.
White, cream or beige breeches.
Black boots.
Gloves.
Spurs.
Whip.

Correct dress for men at advanced and international levels.

Correct Dress for Riders

- It is compulsory for anyone mounted on a horse at a British Dressage affiliated competition to wear a hard hat.
- Under British Dressage rules, BSI standard hats, or such other protective headgear as may reasonably be expected to offer a similar or higher level of protection, are recommended but are not compulsory.
- Men who wear hats secured with chin-straps are not required to remove their hats when saluting.
- Mounted uniform (including uniform hats) may be worn.
- In very hot weather, competitors may be permitted to ride without coats, in which case a suitable shirt (not bright or multi-coloured) must be worn with a tie or hunting tie.
- Gaiters and half-chaps are not permitted.
- Spurs must be of smooth metal, with the shank pointing towards the rear. There is no restriction on the type of shank, and rowels are permitted provided they are fitted vertically. Rowels with points must have rounded ends. Spurs may not be worn upside down.
- Whips may be of any length and are permitted in all national classes except semi-finals, regional championships, other championships or at the request of the selectors.

Correct dress for women at advanced and international levels.

Under Fédération Equestre Internationale (FEI) rules the following dress code applies:

CDIOs *(official international dressage shows)*, *Championships and Regional and Olympic Games*

Top hat.
Black or dark blue tail coat.
Collarless shirt with white hunting tie.
White or off-white breeches.
Black boots.
Gloves.
Spurs.
Whips are not permitted.

CDIs

As above

OR

Bowler hat and black or dark blue coat.

Young Riders

Top hat or bowler hat.
Dark coat.
Collarless shirt with white hunting tie.
White breeches.
Black boots.
Gloves.
Spurs are compulsory.
Whips are not permitted.

Junior Riders

As above, but hunting cap also permitted.
Spurs are optional.
Whips are not permitted.

Pony Riders

Hunting cap.
Dark coat or club uniform coat.
White shirt with ordinary tie or hunting tie.
White or fawn breeches or jodhpurs.
Boots.
Gloves.

Spurs optional. If used, they must be metal, blunt, and must not exceed 1.5cm (½″) in length.
Whips are not permitted.

Pony riders must wear protective headgear whenever mounted.
Pony riders are not permitted to wear a top hat or bowler hat.

- Members of the armed services, police and gendarmerie, members and employees of military establishments and of national studs may wear service dress at all international events.
- Spurs must be metal, with the shank pointing directly back from the centre of the spur. The arms of the spur must be smooth. Rowels, if used, must be free to rotate.

USA

Under AHSA rules, the dress code for training through to Fourth Level is as follows:

Hunt cap or riding hat with a hard shell, derby or top hat.
Short riding coat of conservative colour, with tie, choker or stock tie.
Breeches or jodhpurs.
Boots or jodhpur boots.

For all tests above Fourth Level, the dress code is as follows:

Top hat.
Dark tail coat.
Hunting stock.
White or light coloured breeches.
Black riding boots.
Spurs.

OR

Bowler hat.
Black jacket.
White or light coloured breeches.
Black riding boots.
Spurs.

- One whip, no longer than 4ft (1.2m) including lash, may be carried in all classes except AHSA and USET championships, USET qualifying and selection trials, and observation classes.
- In extreme heat (temperatures above 85 °F (29°C) management may allow competitors to show in the national level classes without jackets. However, competitors must wear solid white long- or short-sleeved shirts without stocks, and regulation hats.
- Competitors will be allowed to wear a hat cover and a transparent or conservative colour raincoat in inclement weather.

7
Endurance Riding

Of all equestrian sports, endurance riding is the one with the least conservative outlook on clothing, the one that most readily embraces new ideas on style, colour and fabrics. No doubt this flexibility has to do with the fact that as an organised, world-wide sport it is of relatively recent origin and therefore not so steeped in tradition as most other equestrian activities. Added to which, at its highest level (for example, at major international championships where horses are required to cover 100 miles in a day) it is unlike any other form of competitive riding.

The physical demands made on riders spending upwards of ten hours in the saddle, often in hot conditions, differ from those in other disciplines, hence the changing fashions within the sport as new designs and new materials come on the market.

For instance, long riding boots may be fine for the lower level of endurance rides but they are less suitable for use over very long distances, particularly since most riders spend some time on their own feet, running beside their horses to give them a breather. Running, especially on uneven ground, calls for a cushioned sole and good ankle support, which is why so many riders have opted for trainer-type footwear.

Footwear of this type, even when specially designed with a heel to provide added safety, is not advised for other forms or riding but it does serve the endurance rider reasonably well. Because trainers 'breathe' they keep the feet relatively cool, though they do have the disadvantage of not being waterproof. For safety's sake, those riders who choose to wear footwear without a suitable heel are required to use an enclosed-type stirrup to guard against the foot slipping right through the iron.

The most popular forms of lower-leg wear are half-chaps or gaiters, which are cooler to wear than riding boots but still afford a good degree of protection.

Traditional jodhpurs or breeches are worn, although again at the higher levels of the sport, riders of both sexes are more likely to be seen wearing ultra-modern riding tights. These very close fitting garments, with padding in strategic places, are said to be the ultimate in comfort for the serious endurance rider.

Comfortable underwear is also absolutely vital. Endurance riders more than any others have benefited from the present-day range of specially designed pants and tops.

Correct Dress for Riders

Riders must give careful consideration to their shirts, too. While T-shirts are permitted at some competitions, it is much more sensible to wear a shirt with a collar and sleeves. Rugby-type shirts provide the best option since they give protection to the back of the neck and to the arms - both important considerations when riding for long periods in the sun, particularly if you are not used to such conditions.

Hats, like footwear, are something of a problem for endurance riders since the jockey skull, so suitable for high-risk sports, can become intolerably heavy and hot when worn for many hours at a stretch. Endurance riders, therefore, are more likely than most to try different types of hat, such as the American-style helmet specifically designed for long spells in the saddle in hot weather. This has a ventilated shell and liner to provide increased airflow, and also a detachable see-through peak. Whichever hat a rider chooses must, of course, give the level of protection laid down in the relevant rule book.

In Britain, endurance riders are encouraged to follow the rules and

Dress for endurance riding is less conservative than in other equestrian sport. Because of the long hours they spend in the saddle, many riders wear American - style helmets which are designed for hot weather.

recommendations laid down by the FEI for international competitions, which are as follows:

- Protective headgear, adequately secured, is compulsory in all endurance competitions. (Cycling-type headgear is not allowed.)

- Dress must be appropriate and not detrimental to the image of endurance riding.

- It is strongly recommended at all endurance competitions, and compulsory at Championships, CEIOs and CEIs, to wear:

Breeches or riding tights with riding boots

OR

Breeches or riding tights with gaiters or half-chaps; or
long socks and ankle-boots or running shoes.

OR

Jodhpurs with ankle boots or running shoes.
Shirt with a collar.

- For ceremonies, a uniform dress is required, comprising helmet, fitted with a silk cover, long-sleeved jacket or wind-breaker, shirt and team tie.
- In inclement weather, appropriate dress may be added.
- If shoes without heels are worn, an enclosed stirrup or other safety stirrup must be used.
- Riding tights must be non-Dayglo earth tone in colour.

In Britain the following also apply:

- A hard hat of PAS015, BSEN 1384, EN1384 or ASTM/SEI standard, with a silk or wide-brimmed cover of the 'hat trick' type, must be worn with the chin-strap securely fastened. It is compulsory for anyone mounted on a horse at any time during an official competition to wear a hard hat with the chin-strap securely fastened.
- Plain chaps are permitted if worn over breeches, jodhpurs or riding trousers.
- A whip may be carried, not exceeding 76.2cm (30″) in length (excluding the thong in the case of a hunting whip).
- Spurs are not permitted.
- It is strongly recommended that earrings, ear-studs, nose-studs and other items of jewellery that might become entangled should not be worn.

8
Horse Trials

The dress for horse trials for men, women and children is based on traditional hunting attire, with modifications for the cross-country phase.
Members of the armed services, police and gendarmerie may wear uniform or civilian dress. Though there is a degree of flexibility within the
term 'hunting attire' (see guidelines to the various levels of competition
below), certain items are included in the sport's rules and are therefore
mandatory.

Safety is of paramount importance, particularly when riding across
country, and riders are urged to wear headgear that passes or surpass-
es the standards currently applicable in their countries. For example, in
Britain a jockey skull (crash hat) should be at least to PAS 015. In the
United States it is the ASTM (American Society for Testing and Materials) that governs hat standards.

In Britain the following rules apply to everyone competing in British
Horse Trials Association (BHTA) official horse trials:

General

Hats

Everyone, competitors or otherwise, riding anywhere at or in the vicinity
of a BHTA official horse trials must wear a hard hat with the harness (if
fitted) correctly fastened. A PAS 015 or EN1384, kitemarked in each
case, jockey skull, or such other protective headgear as may reasonably
be expected to offer a similar or higher level of protection, must be worn
at all times by anyone jumping a horse in the practice areas.

Whips

Whips must not be weighted at the end or exceed 75cm (30″) in length.
It is forbidden to carry a whip while competing in the dressage test,
although a dressage whip may be used while warming up for the test.

Spurs

Spurs are optional except in Advanced and all FEI dressage tests, where they are compulsory. When worn, spurs must be of smooth metal, with a shank no more than 3.5cm (1¼″) long and pointing only towards the rear. If the shank is curved, the spurs must be worn only with the shank directed downwards. The end must be blunt and incapable of wounding a horse. Rowels are not permitted.

Dressage

In the dressage test, riders should wear uniform or hunting dress, including gloves, which may be of any suitable colour.

Cross-country

In the cross-country a crash hat is compulsory. Riders are advised to consider first the PAS015, followed by the EN1384, kitemarked in each case. The harness must be correctly fastened at all times when the rider is mounted. A body protector is also obligatory. BETA classes 2 and 3 are specifically recommended for event riders.

Show jumping

In the show jumping a PAS 015 or EN1384 hat, kitemarked in each case, with a dark blue or black cover, or such other protective headgear as may reasonably be expected to offer a similar or higher level of protection, is compulsory. The harness must be correctly fastened at all times when the rider is mounted.

Juniors

Riders competing in Junior Regional Novice classes and juniors under the age of 16 in Pre-Novice classes may wear jodhpurs and jodhpur boots. All other riders must wear breeches and riding boots.

The recommended dress guidelines (incorporating items governed by the compulsory regulations itemised above) for the various levels of competition are as follows:

Correct dress for the higher levels of horse trials dressage.

Both of these riders are wearing hunting top hats. Some competitors prefer continental-style hats which have a shallower crown.

Women
Dressage

Novice, Pre-Novice and Junior One-Day (but excluding Open Novice)

PAS015 or EN 1384 crash hat, kitemarked in each case, with dark blue
or black cover or dark blue or black hunting cap or bowler hat.
Tweed or dark blue or black coat.
Shirt with collar, and tie with plain bar tie-pin (with tweed coat)

OR

Collarless shirt with coloured hunting tie (with tweed coat) or white
hunting tie (with dark coat).
Breeches (fawn) with plain black or brown boots.
Gloves.

All classes other than Advanced and Intermediate Three-Day,
Advanced One-Day and Intermediate Championship One-Day

PAS015 or EN1384 crash hat, kitemarked in each case, with dark blue
or black cover or dark blue or black hunting cap or bowler hat.
Dark blue or black hunting coat.
Collarless shirt with white hunting tie.
Breeches (fawn) with plain black boots.
Gloves.

Advanced and Intermediate Three-Day Events
Advanced One-Day Horse Trials
Intermediate Championship One-Day Horse Trials

Top hat.
Dark blue or black tail coat.
Collarless shirt with white hunting tie.
Waistcoat (beige, yellow or Tattersall check).
Breeches (fawn) with plain black boots.
Gloves.

Cross-Country

PAS 015 or EN1384 crash hat, kitemarked in each case, with cover in
colour of your own choice.
Long-sleeved sweater or shirt in colour of your own choice.
Hunting tie.
Body protector.
Breeches (fawn) with black boots.

• Brown boots may be worn with fawn breeches in Open Novice,
  Novice, Pre-Novice and Junior one-day horse trials only.

Correct Dress for Riders

Correct dress for the higher levels of horse trials cross-country.

Some riders prefer to wear their body protector over their sweater.

Show Jumping

Novice, Pre-Novice and Junior One-Day (but excluding Open Novice)

PAS 015 or EN1384 hat, kitemarked in each case, with dark blue or black cover.
Tweed or dark blue or black coat.
Shirt with collar, and tie with plain bar tie-pin (with tweed coat)

OR

Collarless shirt with coloured hunting tie (with tweed coat) or white hunting tie (with dark coat).
Breeches (fawn) with plain black or plain brown boots.
Gloves.

All Other Classes

PAS 015 or EN1384 hat, kitemarked in each case, with dark blue or black cover.
Dark blue or black coat.
Collarless shirt with white hunting tie.
Breeches (fawn) with plain black boots.
Gloves.
It is incorrect for ladies to wear white breeches.

Men

Dressage

Novice, Pre-Novice and Junior One-Day only (excluding Open Novice)

PAS015 or EN1384 crash hat, kitemarked in each case, with dark blue or black cover or hunting cap or bowler hat.
Tweed coat.
Shirt with collar, and tie with plain bar tie-pin

OR

Collarless shirt and coloured hunting tie.
Fawn breeches.
Plain black or plain brown boots.
Gloves.

All classes other than Advanced and Intermediate Three-Day, Advanced One-Day and Intermediate Championship One-Day

PAS015 or EN1384 crash hat, kitemarked in each case, with dark blue or black cover or hunting cap or top hat.
Black coat.
Collarless shirt with white hunting tie.
White breeches with black top boots, or fawn breeches with plain black boots.
Gloves.

OR

PAS015 or EN1384 crash hat, kitemarked in each case, with dark blue
or black cover, or hunting cap, or top hat.
Red coat.
Collarless shirt with white hunting tie.
White breeches.
Black boots with brown tops.
Gloves.

Advanced and Intermediate Three-Day Events
Advanced One-Day Horse Trials
Intermediate Championship One-Day Horse Trials

Top hat.
Black or red tail coat.
Collarless shirt with white hunting tie.
Waistcoat (beige or Tattersall check).
White breeches.
Black boots with brown tops.
Gloves.

Cross-Country

PAS 015 or EN1384 crash hat, kitemarked in each case, with cover in
colour of your own choice.
Long-sleeved sweater or shirt in colour of your own choice.
Hunting tie.
Body protector (see rules above).
White breeches and black boots with brown tops, or fawn breeches
with plain black boots.

● Brown boots may be worn with fawn breeches in Open Novice, Novice,
Pre-Novice and Junior one-day horse trials only.

Show Jumping

Novice, Pre-Novice and Junior One-Day only (excluding Open Novice)

PAS 015 or EN1384 hat, kitemarked in each case, with dark blue or
black cover.
Tweed coat.
Shirt with collar, and tie with plain bar tie-pin

OR

Collarless shirt with coloured hunting tie.
Fawn breeches.
Plain black or plain brown boots.
Gloves.

All Other Classes

PAS015 or EN1384 hat, kitemarked in each case,with dark blue or
black cover.

*Correct dress for the higher
levels of horse trials show
jumping*

*In Britain, women wear a
dark blue or black coat, men
wear a red hunting coat (as
above) or black coat.*

69

Black coat.
Collarless shirt with white hunting tie.
White breeches with black boots with brown tops or fawn breeches with plain black boots.
Gloves.

OR

PAS 015 or EN1384 hat, kitemarked in each case, with dark blue or black cover.
Red coat.
Collarless shirt with white hunting tie.
White breeches.
Black boots with brown tops.
Gloves.

• It is incorrect for men to wear fawn breeches with brown-topped boots, or white breeches with plain black boots.

• It is incorrect for women or men to wear earrings.

When competing under Fédération Equestre Internationale (FEI) rules the following regulations apply:

Members of armed and police forces, members and employees of military establishments and national studs must wear service dress with gloves and regulation headgear and spurs (see below). Civilians must wear hunting dress or the uniform of a riding club, with white shirt and tie; gloves; white, fawn or cream breeches; black boots or black boots with brown tops; hunting cap, or top hat, and spurs (see below).

Endurance test

Lightweight clothing is appropriate. Protective headgear (see below) and boots must be worn. It is recommended that body protectors be worn. Spurs are optional (see below).

Show Jumping

Members of armed and police forces, members and employees of military establishments and national studs should wear service dress. Spurs are optional (see below). Civilians must wear hunting dress or the uniform of a riding club, white shirt and tie, white, fawn or cream breeches, black boots or black boots with brown tops. Spurs are optional (see below). All competitors must wear protective headgear (see below).

Protective Headgear

Protective headgear, secured by a permanently fitted, non-detachable retaining harness secured to the shell at more than two points is compulsory for everyone, including grooms, who rides a horse either on the flat or when jumping. (Cycling-type headgear is not allowed.)

Spurs

Spurs capable of wounding a horse are forbidden. Spurs must be of smooth metal. There must be a shank pointing only towards the rear, which must be no more than 3.5cm (1¼″) long and without rowels. The end must be blunt in order to prevent wounding a horse. If the shank is curved, the spurs must be worn only with the shank directed downwards.

Young Riders, Juniors and Pony Riders

The dress code is the same as for seniors, except that pony riders may wear jodhpurs for the cross-country, and spurs, if worn, must be metal and be no longer than 1.5cm (½″). Body protectors are highly recommended.

USA

Dressage

Under AHSA rules the dress code is as follows:

- Uniform or hunting attire, including top hat, hunting cap or regulation headgear.
  Spurs, which are not capable of wounding a horse, are required above Preliminary level. Rowel spurs are not permitted.

- Members and employees of military establishments, national studs and police forces should wear service dress, with regulation headgear and spurs. Spurs must be of smooth metal. There must be a shank pointing only towards the rear, which must be no more than 3.5cm long and without rowels. The end must be blunt in order to prevent wounding a horse. If the shank is curved, the spurs must be worn only with the shank directed downwards.

- In extreme temperature conditions the Ground Jury has the option to allow competitors to compete without jackets. In such cases, competitors must wear solid white long- or short-sleeved shirts.

Cross-Country

Under AHSA rules the dress code, including regulations governing the dimensions of spurs and whips, is the same as in Britain. Protective headgear with harness secured is obligatory when jumping a fence on the course or in the warm-up areas. The AHSA strongly encourages all riders to wear protective headgear passing or surpassing current applicable ASTM (American Society for Testing and Materials) standards.

9
Hunting

There are no mandatory rules for what to wear when riding to hounds, but the dress adopted by the different categories of rider at various times of year does follow a well-defined pattern. There are, in fact, what might be called 'unwritten laws'.

In the early part of the autumn hunting season (August/September) dress is fairly informal. It is known as 'ratcatcher'. As the autumn season progresses and the opening meet draws nearer, clothes generally become smarter. For the opening meet and thereafter, full hunting dress, as itemised below, is worn.

The rules for dress are governed by the rider's status in the hunt. Masters and hunt servants wear the official hunt uniform, which may consist of red, green or other coloured coat with hunt button and distinctive collar, or facings, if applicable.

With the exception of farmers over whose land the hunt goes, any rider who regularly hunts with a pack of hounds must become a subscriber. If you live in hunting country and have subscribed to the hunt over a certain period, you may be invited by the Master to wear the hunt's distinctive button, thus becoming a member. You are then entitled to wear the hunt button and, sometimes, a distinctive collar and facings. Until then, your black coat should have plain black buttons. Or it is correct to wear a red coat with plain brass or regimental buttons.

If you are in any doubt, check with the hunt exactly what dress is considered correct.

Generally speaking, hunting clothes are designed for comfort, to keep the wearer warm and dry, to give protection from the inevitable knocks received when riding across country, and to look neat and tidy.

Hats

In times gone by it was the prerogative of Masters, hunt servants and farmers to wear black hunting caps. Masters and hunt servants wore their caps with the ribbons at the back hanging down, while farmers wore caps without ribbons (this is not just a question of fashion – it makes it easier instantly to recognise the status of the persons concerned). Male subscribers or members wore top hats, as did ladies riding side-saddle. Ladies riding astride wore bowlers.

Eventually women gave up bowler hats for hunting caps, and resolved the problem of the ribbons by cutting off the parts that hang down, or by sewing them up. A further change came about when men began to accept that top hats were not the best means of protecting their heads. As a result, more and more male subscribers and members began to wear hunting caps.

Nowadays it is generally acceptable for anyone riding to hounds to wear a hunting cap or, indeed, a crash hat, complete with harness.

The following are still the traditionally accepted modes of dress for hunting in Britain – but remember that the PAS 015 crash hat (or such other suitable protective headgear as may reasonably be expected to offer a similar or higher level of protection) worn with a correctly fitted chin-harness, will give better protection than the traditional top hat or bowler.

Autumn hunting (early part of season)

Men and ladies riding astride PAS 015 crash hat with cover, or hunting cap, or bowler hat. Whipcord or tweed coat, usually brown or greenish.
Fawn or drab breeches.
Black or brown boots with garter straps.
Hunting whip with thong and lash or cutting whip with hunting-whip handle but no thong.
Gloves.
Spurs.

Ladies riding side-saddle

Hunting cap or when the season opens, top hat on Saturday and for lawn meets or bowler hat with veil.
Black or blue habit, with hunt buttons.
Collarless shirt with white hunting tie and plain bar tie-pin.
Waistcoat.
Black boots.
Gloves.
Spurs.
Whip.

Autumn hunting (later part of season)

As above, but shirt with collar and tie may be replaced by dark-coloured hunting tie.

Correct Dress for Riders

Correct dress for a woman when autumn hunting. Many riders now wear a crash hat with harness and silk or velvet cover.

Correct dress for a man when autumn hunting. A crash hat is now often considered preferable to a bowler.

For both men and women, fawn breeches and plain black boots are worn with a black coat.

Formal hunting dress for men consists of a red hunting coat worn with either a top hat or hunting cap. The rider on the left is wearing a cut-away coat.

In this picture the rider is wearing a standard hunting coat.

The rider in this picture is wearing a hunting cap with a standard red coat. Nowadays many riders wear either a hat with a harness, or a crash hat.

Opening meet and throughout season

Hunt members

Women

PAS 015 crash hat with cover, or hunting cap (with ribbons cut or sewn up) or bowler hat.
Dark blue or black coat, with appropriate collar and buttons.
Collarless shirt with white or cream hunting tie and plain bar tie-pin.
Waistcoat or dark V-necked sweater.
Fawn breeches.
Black boots with garter straps.
Gloves.
Hunting whip or cutting whip.
Spurs.

- Hunting coats should be in a warm (34oz) material. Ladies may wear two vents, men only one. The lining should be fawn or dark, not brightly coloured.

A man's hunting coat should have a long two-button vent with a seam at the waist.

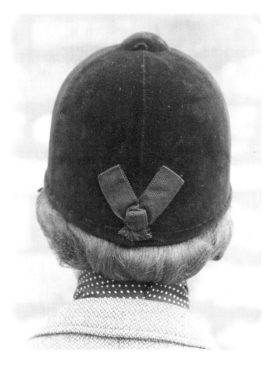

If you wear a hunting cap, cut off the ribbons at the back, or tuck them up

78

Men

PAS 015 crash hat with cover or hunting cap (with ribbons cut or sewn up) or top hat.
Red coat with rounded front and three or four hunt buttons; or red or black swallowtail coat or black coat.
Collarless shirt with white hunting tie, and plain bar tie-pin.
Waistcoat (yellow, beige or Tattersall check).
White breeches and black boots with brown tops and white garter straps (with red coat). Or fawn breeches and plain black boots and black garter straps (with black coat).
Gloves.
Hunting whip or cutting whip.
Spurs.

● The hunting coat should be made of good, thick material, correctly cut, and should have two buttons on the back of the 'skirt', with a long vent and a seam at the waist.

❏ White breeches are not worn with plain boots.
❏ Fawn breeches are not worn with brown-topped boots.
❏ White breeches and brown-topped boots may be worn with a black coat.
❏ If you wear a hunting cap, remember to cut off the ribbons or tuck or sew them up.

● Gloves should be warm and provide good grip on the reins in wet weather. They should be the same colour as the breeches.

● A hunting whip with a bone or horn handle and a thong and lash is more useful out hunting than an ordinary whip. The handle helps when opening and shutting gates. The thong and lash will help keep hounds clear of your horse's legs. The thong can also be used to form a loop, providing a useful aid for capturing a loose, bridle-less horse. Alternatively, a cutting whip with a hunting-whip handle but no thong may be carried.

NB Other than with foxhounds, red or scarlet coats are not worn by anyone except Masters and hunt servants. For stag hunting, only black coats or ratcatcher are worn.

10
Hunter Trials And Team Chasing

Hunter Trials

PAS 015 crash hat with dark blue or black cover.
Body protector of BETA Class 3 (purple lable).
Tweed coat.
Collarless shirt with dark-coloured hunting tie.
Fawn breeches.
Plain boots with garter straps.

Children: tweed coat, shirt and tie with jodhpurs and jodhpur boots.

Gloves.

OR

PAS 015 crash hat with cover in colour of your own choice.
Body protector of BETA Class 3 (purple lable).
Long-sleeved sweater in colour of your own choice. Very bright colours are not considered suitable for hunter trials.
White hunting tie.
Fawn breeches.
Plain boots with garter straps.

Children: shirt and tie with jodhpurs and jodhpur boots.
Gloves.

Team Chasing

Team chasing is a very relaxed sport, with few mandatory rules. However, those who take part recognise the inherent dangers of riding at speed over fixed obstacles, and invariably adopt the safest clothing available. A crash hat to the highest possible standard, worn with a correctly secured harness, is the only sensible form of headgear. Body protectors are also highly recommended. Otherwise, dress normally complies with the cross-country version worn for hunter trials (see above). Team members usually wear the same matching colours.

Initially an adult sport, team chasing now attracts riders in their late teens. It is not, however, recommended for Pony Club branches.

11
Point-to-Pointing

Point-to-pointing, like all forms of racing, is a high-risk sport, and the rules on dress concentrate on safety aspects. A correctly fitted jockey skull cap to BSEN 1384: 1997 or EN1384: 1996 or PAS 015: 1994 standard is mandatory. Skull caps, cradle or draw lace. The chin-strap must pass under the jaw and be attached to the harness by a quick release buckle. Metal hooks are expressly forbidden. A body protector is also mandatory. No one may ride in spectacles or vision-corrected goggles.

The other items of dress traditionally worn for race-riding are as listed below. Black lightweight racing boots with brown tops are worn, with white breeches, by both sexes. However, fawn breeches and black boots are sometimes worn. Most point-to-point riders wear sweaters, which give protection against the cold. Racing silks are also worn, particularly by heavier riders needing to keep their overall weight down as much as possible. A white hunting tie is correct with silks and it is advisable to wear one under a sweater, too, as protection for the neck in the event of a fall.

Unless you expect to ride in hunter chases (in which case the owner's colours must be registered with the Jockey Club) there is no need to register racing colours for point-to-pointing.

Most race-riders wear gloves; the extra grip which they provide on the reins is often vital when riding a sweaty or rain-soaked horse, especially if he is a hard puller. Many riders favour the fingerless variety, which provide grip, and warmth, without restricting the hands.

Dress for Men and Women

BSEN 1384, EN 1384 or PAS 015 jockey skull with harness, and coloured cover.
Body protector of a pattern approved by the stewards of the Jockey Club.
Polo necked sweater or racing silks with white hunting tie.
White breeches.
Black racing boots with brown tops.
Gloves.
Under the rules of Point-to-Pointing the following details apply:

Skull Caps

It is obligatory for riders to wear correctly-fitted skullcaps, with the harness correctly adjusted and fastened, at all times when mounted. Any skull cap that has been subjected to severe impact should be discarded, and any rider who has suffered concussion must discard the skull cap which he or she was wearing at the time.

At race meetings, point-to-point doctors and Jockey Club officials may make random inspections of skull caps.

Correct dress for point-to-pointing (men and women).

Whips

Whips must not exceed 68cm (27″) in length, including the flap, and must be no less than 1cm (3/8″) in diameter. The flap may be no more than 10cm (3 7/8″) long from the end of the shaft and must be no less than 2cm (3/4″) wide and no more than 4cm (1 5/8″) wide. Flaps which contain re- inforcements or additions are not permitted. There must be no binding within 23cm (9″) of the end of the flaps. The flap must be covered by felt or other similar material and must not be closed. Random checks of whips may be made by Clerks of the Scales as riders leave the weighing room for the parade ring, and also by the Stewards in the parade ring.

Spectacles and Contact Lenses

In the interests of safety, no one riding in a point-to-point may wear spectacles or vision-corrected goggles. If contact lenses are worn, they must be of the soft or perma type.

Spurs

Spurs are permitted, but they must not be sharp, angled, or fitted with rowels.

Point-to-Point rider correctly dressed.

12
Polo

The rules of polo (Hurlingham Polo Association) provide only a brief guide to dress requirements, though players invariably wear the same traditional turnout in competitions. The one compulsory item is a helmet, which in Britain should be PAS 015 or EN1384.

For matches and tournaments the following is the normal turnout for men and women:
  Polo helmet, which must be worn with a chin-strap.
  White breeches.
  Brown boots.
  Knee pads (optional).
  Team shirt.
  Gloves. Leather or (for wet weather) non-slip.
Note also:

Helmets

Umpires, as well as players, must wear a polo helmet or cap with a chin-strap. Goal judges are also required to wear a safety helmet. No one may ride on polo grounds or their vicinities without a hard hat.

Boots and knee pads

Players must not wear buckles or studs on the upper part of their boots, or knee pads in such a way that could damage another player's boots or breeches.

Spurs

Spurs, if worn, must not be sharp. The shank, which must point towards the rear, should be no more than 3cm (1¹/4″) long including any rowel. If the shank is curved or angled, the spurs must be worn with the shank directed downwards.

Whips

Whips must not exceed 122cm (48″) in length, including any tag. Broken whips are not allowed.

Correct dress for polo (men and women).

A helmet with a correctly fitting chin-strap is compulsory.

Close-up showing correct knee and leg protection.

Practice chukkas

Most clubs permit riders to practise in informal attire such as jeans, with or without leather chaps. All players should have a white shirt and two shirts in the colour of their club. Brown or black boots may be worn.

NB For correct dress for Pony Club members, see *Chapter 5*.

13
Show Jumping

Show jumping dress at both national and international level is derived from hunting dress: the only exception being that members of the armed services, police, military establishments and national studs may wear uniform if they wish.

In line with developments in other equestrian sports, some national federations now take the wearing of safe headgear far more seriously than they used to. In Britain, for example, it is mandatory for riders to wear a hat with a correctly fitted and fastened chin-strap when jumping in the arena, the practice area and the collecting ring.

Under international rules, however, the wearing of a harness is not (at the time of writing) mandatory for adults although it is recommended for young riders and compulsory for juniors and children.

BSJA Requirements

When competing under British Show Jumping Association (BSJA) rules the following dress is correct for larger shows:

Adults and Juniors

Protective headgear with retaining harness secured to shell at more than two points.

Tailored riding jacket.

A white or pastel coloured shirt with collar and white tie, or a white collarless shirt with white hunting tie, is compulsory with a blue, black, red or green coat. Women may wear high-collared white or pastel coloured show jumping shirts without a tie or hunting tie. Junior BSJA members who are also Pony Club members may wear Pony Club ties whatever the colour of their coat.

Breeches or jodhpurs (white, pale yellow or fawn).

Plain black riding boots (men and women) or black boots with brown tops (men) or jodhpur boots. Plain black leather (not suede) 'gaiters' cut in the traditional riding boot style may be worn with black jodhpur boots, but not when red coats are compulsory.

At international and major national shows, men wear a black, red, green or blue coat with a white collar and tie and top boots.

Correct dress for women is as for men, but with plain black boots.

13 Show Jumping

- The BSJA strongly recommends the wearing of a protective helmet manufactured to BSEN 1384 (which in the arena must be worn with a plain-coloured peaked cover) or a riding cap to BSEN 1384, or such other suitable protective headgear as a similar or higher level of protection and is at least that of BSEN 1384. Hats must be worn with the chinstrap correctly adjusted and fastened when jumping in the arena, practice area and collecting ring.
- Body protectors, if worn by adults, must be worn under jackets. Junior members may wear body protectors either underneath or over their jackets.
- Competitors may wear the identification (name and / or logo) of the manufacturer of clothing requirement or, as an alternative, that of a sponsor. Full details are to be found in the current rule book.
- In hot weather competitors may be permitted to compete without jackets, at the judges' discretion, in which case they must wear white shirts with long or short sleeves. Ties must be firmly secured. Braces may not be worn.
- At prize-givings, competitors are required to be mounted and correctly dressed. Failure to do so may incur elimination.
- On wet days the judges may allow riders to wear mackintoshes when competing and when walking the course.
- Competitors must at all times wear correct riding clothes, including jacket, whenever they enter the arena, except on very hot days when the judges may permit riders to carry their jackets during the course-walk.

Spurs. Spurs, if worn, must be fitted with the neck of the spur pointing downwards. Excessively severe designs are not permitted: these include spurs with necks more than 3cm 1 ($^1/_4$") long; necks set on the inside of the heel; rowel diameters of more than 1cm ($^1/_2$"); roughened or cutting edges and serrated spurs, with or without necks. In pony competitions only blunt spurs, with necks not exceeding 2cm ($^3/_4$") in length, are permitted. Plastic spurs are not allowed.

Whips. No rider may carry, use or permit to be used a whip greater than 75cm (2' 3") or less than 45cm (1' 5") in length overall nor one which is weighted or with a hard point at the end in the arena, the collecting ring or anywhere in the immediate vicinity of the showground. No substitute for a whip may be carried in any competition. Whips, if carried, should be carried at all times in the hand. Juniors may carry a whip not exceeding 65 cms (2' 1")in length.

FEI Requirements

When competing under Fédération Equestre Internationale (FEI) rules the following regulations apply:

Adults, Young Riders and Juniors

Civilians should wear the dress approved by their national federation: red or black coat, breeches (white for men, white or fawn for women), hunting cap, plain black boots or black boots with brown tops. A hunting tie is recommended for international events, otherwise a white shirt and tie, or cravat (choker) must be worn.

The wearing of a hard hat is compulsory for all riders (including grooms) when jumping a horse.

Adults and young riders. It is strongly recommended that anyone working a horse in the exercise and schooling areas or anywhere on the show ground should wear a hard hat.

It is compulsory for juniors and children to wear protective head gear secured by a three-point retention harness when mounted.

If wearing a chin-strap, male riders are not required to remove their hats when saluting.

Riders must wear correct dress when competing and during the presentation of prizes.

During inclement weather, the Ground Jury may permit competitors to wear waterproofs.

When walking the course, riders must be neat and tidy and must wear riding boots, white shirt and white tie.

Members of the armed services, police and gendarmerie, members and employees of military establishments and of national studs may compete in service dress BUT it is compulsory for anyone wearing service dress to *wear a hard hat when jumping.*

Pony Riders

Protective headgear secured by a three-point retention harness is compulsory at all times when mounted.

Dark coat or club uniform coat.

White collarless shirt with white hunting tie, or white shirt with collar and white tie.

White or fawn breeches or jodhpurs.

Riding boots or jodhpur boots.

Spurs - optional. If worn, they must be of blunt metal and must not exceed 1.5cm (½″) in length.

Instead of a white collar and tie or hunting tie, some women wear a white shirt with a round collar.

It is permissible for servicemen to wear uniform.

- A competitor who loses his or her hat, or whose harness becomes unfastened during the round, must stop and replace/refasten it. There is no penalty, even if the rider has to dismount, but the clock will not be stopped.
- A competitor who jumps or attempts to jump an obstacle or who passes through the finish with his or her hat-harness incorrectly fastened will be eliminated, unless the Ground Jury decides that they were so far committed that they could not be expected to pull up before attempting to jump or to go through the finish.

Whips. Competitors are allowed to use a dressage whip when working on the flat but are strictly forbidden to use or carry a whip which is weighted at the end at any time or to carry or use one which is more than 75cm (2′ 3″)in length in the arena, exercise or schooling areas when riding over poles or any obstacle. No substitute for a whip may be carried.

Pony riders are forbidden to carry or use a whip more than 75cm (2′ 3″) in length, or one that is weighted at the end, in the arena, the exercise and schooling areas or anywhere on or in the immediate vicinity of the showground. No substitute for a whip may be carried.

USA

Under AHSA rules, in senior classes offering $25,000 or more in prize money only black, dark blue, dark green or scarlet coats are permitted.

Junior and Children's Hunter Division

Under AHSA rules, riders are required to wear formal hunting attire, with protective headgear. Junior riders may only wear brown boot-tops with a scarlet coat. Hunt colours may be worn in classes restricted to members, subscribers or staff of a hunt recognized by the Master of Foxhounds Association. All riders who wear colours must carry a letter dated within the current year signifying that they are eligible. The letter must include the name of the hunt and the colour of the collar and must be signed by the Master or Honorary Secretary of that hunt.

- Under AHSA rules, riders in all classes where jumping is required, and when jumping on the showgrounds, must wear protective head gear. (Exception: trail classes.)

14
Showing

The overall aim in showing classes is for the rider to complement the horse or pony rather than to detract from it. It is, after all, the animal who is being judged not the rider. Therefore bright colours (including coat linings), large buttonholes, jewellery and heavy make-up should all be avoided.

When tying on your number, always use a cord or ribbon of the same colour as your coat. This looks much neater than the ribbon (usually light coloured) supplied with the number.

Hair should be neat and tidy, with no fringe showing at the front. Men look better if their hair is not too long at the back. Women with anything other than a short haircut should tie their hair back or wear a hairnet. Girls' hair ribbons should be kept to a minimum. Again, bright colours should be avoided.

As in other equestrian sports, safe headgear is now much more commonly seen in the show ring than in the past. Indeed, in the jumping phase of working hunter classes a PAS 015 or BS 4472 crash hat or a BS 6473 hunting cap with correctly fitted chin-strap must be worn.

The correct dress for the various classes is as follows:

Adults

Men

Hunters, working hunters, riding horses, cobs and hacks
Bowler hat (except for the jumping phase of working hunter classes, when a PAS 015 or BS 4472 skull cap with dark blue or black cover, or BS 6473 hunting cap, both with correctly fastened chin-strap, must be worn).
Tweed coat.
Shirt with collar, and tie with plain bar tie-pin.
Fawn or buff breeches.
Plain black or brown boots with garter straps.
Leather or string gloves.
Plain or leather-covered show cane not exceeding 1m (39″) in length.
Spurs.

In show classes for hunters, riding horses, cobs and hacks, men wear a tweed coat with a bowler hat (above left). Women wear a black, blue or tweed coat with a hunting cap or bowler hat (above, right). For showing riding horses, but not hunters, a tweed coat with velvet collar is acceptable (left).

For hack classes at major shows, men wear a morning coat, black riding trousers and a top hat.

Hunters and working hunters at London and international shows

Daytime: Dress as on page 93.

Evening:
Top hat.
Red or black hunting coat, either ordinary pattern or cut away.
Collarless shirt with white hunting tie.
White breeches (with red or black coat) and boots with brown tops and white garter straps

OR

Fawn or buff breeches with plain black boots.
Leather or string gloves.
Hunting whip.
Spurs.

Correct Dress for Riders

Cobs and riding horses at London and international shows

Daytime: Dress as on page 93.

Evening:
  Top hat.
  Red or black hunting coat, either ordinary pattern or cut away.
  Collarless shirt with white hunting tie.
  White breeches (with red coat) and boots with mahagony tops and white garter straps

OR

  White breeches and black patent top boots (with black coat)

OR

  Fawn or buff breeches and plain black boots.
  Leather or string gloves.
  Hunting whip.
  Spurs.

When riding cobs at major shows, some ladies prefer to wear a top hat and hunting tie.

Hacks at London and international shows

Daytime: Dress as on page 93.

Evening:
Black morning coat with tight-fitting black riding trousers, and shirt with collar and tie or cravat.

Women

Hunters, working hunters, riding horses, cobs and hacks

Bowler hat or hunting cap (except for the jumping phase of working hunter classes, when a PAS 015 or BS 4472 skull cap with dark blue or black cover or BS 6473 hunting cap, both with correctly fitted chin-strap, must be worn).
Tweed or dark blue or black coat.
Shirt with collar, and tie with plain bar tie-pin.
Fawn or buff breeches.
Plain black or brown boots with garter straps.
Leather or string gloves.
Plain or leather-covered show cane not exceeding 1m (39″) in length.
Spurs.
Buttonholes may be worn in hack classes but should be extremely small.

Hunters and working hunters at London and international shows

Daytime: Dress as on page 93.

Evening:
Bowler hat or hunting cap.
Dark blue or black hunting coat.
Collarless shirt with white hunting tie.
Fawn breeches.
Plain black boots with garter straps.
Leather or string gloves.
Hunting whip.
Spurs.

Cobs and riding horses at London and international shows

Daytime: Dress as above.

Evening:
Bowler hat or hunting cap. Some women wear top hats.
Dark blue or black coat.
Fawn breeches.
Plain black boots with garter straps.
Leather or string gloves.
Hunting whip.
Spurs.

Hacks at London and international shows

Morning: Dress as on page 93.

Evening:
Bowler hat, hunting cap or top hat.
Dark blue or black coat.
Collarless shirt with white hunting tie.
Fawn breeches.
Plain black boots.

Side-saddle: hunters, working hunters, riding horses and hacks

Bowler hat with veil.
Hair in a bun (false if necessary).
Dark blue or black habit with black boots.
Shirt with collar, and tie with plain bar tie-pin.
Leather gloves.
Cane or whip not more than 1m (39″) in length.

Royal shows

Dress as above.

OR

Top hat with veil.
White hunting tie.

London shows

Daytime: Dress as above.

Evening:
Top hat with veil.
White hunting tie.

- The National Light Horse Breeding Society (HIS) rules specify that spurs must be of smooth metal, with a shank not exceeding 3.5cm in length and pointing only towards the rear. Rowels are not permitted. The end must be blunt and incapable of wounding a horse. If the shank is curved, the spurs must be worn with the shank directed downwards.

Mountain and Moorland Ponies

PAS 015 or BS 4472 crash hat, with velvet cover in a colour that tones in with the coat; or BS 6473 hunting cap. A crash hat must be worn in working hunter pony classes.
Tweed coat.
Shirt with collar, and tie with plain bar tie-pin. A hunting tie may be worn in working hunter pony classes.
Fawn or cream breeches.

Plain black boots.
String or leather gloves.
Spurs (optional).
Leather-covered show cane.

NB: If a cane is carried, it must comply with the rules of the appropriate breed society or the national rules, as applicable.

*When showing horses side-saddle, women wear either a bowler hat
with veil (see inset), and a collar and tie (above left), or a top hat
and hunting tie, depending on the type of show and the time of day
(above right).*

Children

Show Ponies

British Standards crash hat (with dark blue or black cover) or dark blue or black hunting cap numbers EN1384, PAS015, BS 4472 or 6473 or PAS accredited hat.
Dark blue or brown coat.
Shirt with collar, and tie with plain bar tie-pin.
Cream or fawn jodhpurs.
Brown jodhpur boots.
Leather gloves (string gloves are also acceptable).
Small buttonholes may be worn.
Plain or leather-covered show cane.

Ponies of Show Hunter Type and Working Hunter Ponies

British Standards crash hat (with dark blue or black cover) or dark blue or black hunting cap numbers EN1384, PAS015, BS 4472 or 6473 or PAS accredited hat.
Tweed coat. (Dark blue or black coats may be worn for final judging at major shows.)
Shirt with collar, and tie with plain bar tie-pin.
Fawn jodhpurs.
Brown jodhpur boots. For older children, plain riding boots with garter straps.
Cane or whip not exceeding 75cm (30″) in length. (Hunting whips are permitted.)

- No spurs.

Side-saddle

PAS 015 or BS 4472 crash hat with dark blue or black cover, or dark blue or black BS 6473 hunting cap.
Side-saddle habit with black riding boots.
Shirt with collar, and tie with plain bar tie-pin.
Leather gloves.
Cane or whip not more than 75cm (30″) in length.

- Hair ribbons should be black, brown or navy blue only, and should be kept to a minimum.
- It is incorrect for children riding side-saddle in showing classes to wear a spur.

Mountain and Moorland Ponies

PAS 015 or BS 4472 crash hat, with a velvet cover that tones in with the colour of the coat; or BS 6473 hunting cap. A crash hat must be worn in working hunter pony classes.
Tweed coat.
Shirt with collar, and tie with plain bar tie-pin.
Fawn or cream jodhpurs with brown jodhpur boots (younger riders).

A child correctly dressed for showing ponies of show hunter type or working hunter ponies.

Girls showing ponies side-saddle wear a crash hat with dark cover, or a hunting cap.

OR

Fawn or cream breeches with plain black boots.
String or leather gloves.
Leather-covered show cane.

Under British Show Pony Society (BSPS) rules, the following apply:

- It is compulsory for riders to wear a correctly secured British Standard skull cap/riding hat numbers EN1384, PAS015, BS 4472 or 6473 or PAS accredited hat at all times when mounted. A rider whose hat comes off or becomes unfastened must replace/refasten it before continuing.
- Whips must not exceed 75cm (30") in length.
- Body protectors may be worn.
- The wearing of spurs in all classes is forbidden.
- Earrings should not be worn.

Correct dress for (left) an adult and (right) a child in ridden moutain and moorland pony classes.

NB With the exception of certain rules governing hats, whips and spurs, there are few mandatory requirements in the showing world, although it is customary to follow the guidelines detailed above. If you are in any doubt as to what to wear for a particular class, consult the society or association under whose rules the class or show is being judged. Or watch the experts - they usually get it right!

USA

Under AHSA rules the dress code is as follows:

Hunter Seat Equitation

Conservative coloured protective headgear.
Tweed or Melton coat (conservative wash-jackets permitted in season).
Breeches or jodhpurs.
Riding or jodhpur boots.
Spurs, crops or bats optional.

Hunter Division

Hunting cap, derby or hunting silk hat.
Scarlet or dark coat.
White shirt with white stock.
White, buff or canary breeches.

● Hunt colours may be worn in classes restricted to members, subscribers or staff of a hunt recognized by the Masters of Foxhounds Association. All riders who wear colours must carry a letter dated within the current year signifying that they are eligible. The letter must include the name of the hunt and the colour of the collar, and must be signed by the Master or Honorary Secretary of that hunt.

Under the regulations of the American Horse Shows Association (AHSA) all juniors riding in hunter, jumper and hunter seat equitation sections must wear properly fitting protective headgear while riding in the designated schooling and exercise areas, the show ring and while jumping anywhere on the competition grounds.

The AHSA strongly encourages all riders to wear protective headgear passing or surpassing current applicable ASTM (American Society for Testing and Materials)/SEI (Safety Equipment Institute) standards with harness secured while riding anywhere on the competition grounds.

Boots/shoes worn while riding anywhere on the competition grounds must have a distinguishable heel. (Exception: Arabian, Hackney Pony, Morgan, National Show Horse, Parade, Roadster, Saddlebred and Saddle Seat Equitation.)

15
Side-Saddle

During the last few decades there has been a significant revival of interest in side-saddle riding all over the world: especially in Europe, the United States, Canada, Australia, New Zealand and Japan.

Competitions available to side-saddle riders include show classes, concours d'élégance, show jumping and dressage. Generally speaking, correct side-saddle attire is acceptable in all these activities, but riders must be careful to study the rules of the Society under which individual competitions are run, to ensure that they comply with any special requirements. For instance, under BSJA rules, side-saddle riders must wear the correct safety headgear.

Equitation classes and championships, in which horse and rider are judged on both performance and turnout, are popular. In Britain they are run under the auspices of the Side-Saddle Association, which gives the following guidelines for turnout. (note that the riders dress is determined by the type of hat worn):

Adults
Adult wearing a bowler/BS standard hat

Safety bowler hat with a veil, or hat to at least, BS 4472 or BS 6473 standard without a veil.
Habit in a restrained colour, with long black boots.

OR

Tweed or discreet check (e.g. Prince of Wales) habit, with long black or brown boots according to colour of habit.
Garter straps are optional.
Plain, or discreetly striped, shirt with collar and tie, and plain bar tie-pin.
Breeches of a colour similar to or the same as that of the habit. (If light-coloured breeches are worn they must not show at any time.)
Waistcoat.
Brown or tan leather or string gloves.
Whip or rigid cane no more than 1m (39″) in length.
Blunt spur or spur band, to be worn on counter (seam) of boot.

Mounted rider in correct habit, with bowler hat.

Dismounted rider in correct habit, with silk top hat. The apron is secured for ease when walking.

OR

Adult wearing a silk hat

Silk hat with a veil. The height of the crown should measure between 120mm (4 ^{3}/$_4$″) and 133mm (5 ^{1}/$_4$″), depending on the height of the wearer.

Habit, in a restrained colour, with long black boots.

Garter straps are optional.

Collarless shirt with plain hunting tie (stock).
Breeches.
Waistcoat.
Dark brown or tan leather or cream chamois leather gloves.
Whip.
Spur.

- Brightly-coloured waistcoats, such as red, should not be worn.
- It is incorrect to wear floral buttonholes, earrings, or other visible jewellery.
- It is incorrect to wear black gloves.
- Side-Saddle Association badges may be worn.
- If a dressage whip is carried, it should be leather-covered and the end tassel should not be of a bright colour.
- Hair should be worn in a bun (false, if necessary) and should be held in a fine mesh hairnet of the same colour as the hair.

Juniors (aged under 16 on the previous 1 January)

As for adults wearing a bowler hat except:
Crash hat to at least BS 4472 or BS 6473, hunting cap or safety bowler (all without a veil) must be worn. Hunting cap ribbons should be stitched up inside the cap.
A spur or spur band is not compulsory.
Hair ribbons, if worn, must be plain black, brown or navy.
Hair, however worn, should be exceptionally neat and tidy.
Whip not to exceed 75cm (30") in length.
Jodhpur boots are acceptable in the case of small children.

USA

Under AHSA rules the dress code for ladies riding side-saddle is as follows:

Black hunting silk hat at least 4 1/2" (115mm) high without adornments.

A hunt cap is permissible for jumping classes.
Traditional black veil.
Habit in Melton or other cloth of black or dark blue colour, unless the rider is a bona fide member of a recognized hunt whose livery colour is different, then hunt livery colour with hunt colours is permissible.
Lining must match.
Plain white hunting stock, with plain gold safety pin worn horizontally.
Breeches in the same colour as the habit.

- The collar should be in the same material and colour as the coat unless the member has been invited to wear the hunt colours, in which case the collar should conform to the livery of the hunt and be worn only on coats of the hunt livery colour.

16
Riding Club Activities

Members of the many riding clubs affiliated to the British Horse Society have a wide range of organised activities in which to take part. In general, dress requirements for each activity correspond with those laid down for the appropriate disciplines when run under BHS rules. The chief exception is the use of whips, which are not permitted in some competitions under riding club rules: for example in dressage and in the dressage test in horse trials. Be sure to check the rules in advance.

Safety is a prime consideration and the general recommendations discussed in *Chapter 2*, concerning hats, footwear, hair, etc, all apply.

For rallies and instructional rides, members are expected to be neat and tidy. Jeans are not acceptable but dark coloured breeches or jodhpurs are. Shirts or polo-necked sweaters may be worn. Riders are advised not to wear short-sleeved garments.

Spurs, when worn, must be metal, and must not have a neck exceeding 3cm (1¼″) in length. Rowels and roughened or serrated spurs are not permitted. If the neck of the spur curves, the spur must only be worn with the curve directed downwards. Spurs are permitted in dressage, show jumping and cross-country but not in riding-test competitions or in equitation jumping or endurance riding.

● The dress requirements for the teams-of-three competition, which is unique to riding clubs, are basically the same as for hunting, though the following points should be noted:

PAS 015 or BS 4472 crash hat with dark blue or black cover or BS 6473 hunting cap must be worn.
Whips, if carried, should be not less than 45cm (18″) and no more than 75cm (30″) in length. Hunting whips are not recommended.
Buttonholes and brightly-coloured hair ribbons are not acceptable.

As well as competitions, training is also an important part of the Riding Clubs movement. Candidates for the various Grade Tests and examinations should be correctly turned out, partly out of courtesy to the examiner but also to demonstrate that they understand the basics of safe dress. For the lower grade tests, nothing too formal is required: jodhpurs and jodhpur boots and club sweatshirts are usually acceptable. The higher up the scale you go the more formal the dress requirements become. When applying for entry to any of the examinations, including the stable management phases, check with the Riding Clubs' rules to make sure you know what is required.

17
Grooms

Working as a groom is a responsible job. You are responsible, in varying degrees (depending on your level of experience), for the safety and well-being of someone else's often valuable animals; and for much of the time you are also responsible for your own safety. When working with horses, whether on the ground, in the saddle or in transit, there is always going to be some element of danger because of the sheer size and unpredictability of the animals concerned. Responsible grooms will, therefore, take every precaution not to put themselves, or the horses or ponies in their care, at risk through inattention to basic safety precautions when it comes to what to wear at work.

While casual clothes such as jeans and sweatshirts are perfectly acceptable, the same safety rules that apply to everyone working with horses also apply to grooms. In fact, safety is of particularly vital importance since grooms often spend far more hours each day with their charges than the owners do – and frequently they find themselves handling unfamiliar animals.

Grooming can be hard, and on occasions dirty, work. Depending on the type of yard in which you are employed, there may be times when you are required to be outside in all types of weather. Good, strong, hard-wearing clothes are therefore essential, as are ones that will stand up to being thrown into the washing machine over and over again.

Responsible employers will ensure that you wear appropriate, safe dress both when working in the stables and when riding. When you are working without supervision it is up to you to adhere to the tried and tested safety guidelines outlined below. Indeed, they should become second nature to you.

Remember, too, that if you work with competition horses, you must conform to the rules of your particular sport when on the showground. For example, it is now mandatory in most disciplines for anyone – i.e. rider or groom – to wear a correctly fitted hard hat at all times when mounted.

When setting off for a competition for the first time, be sure to check with your employer, or another more experienced groom, what you will need to take with you.

As well as being safe, to be neatly turned out is also courteous to your employer and – if you are working with competition horses or in a training centre – to the public. Always start the day with clean clothes and boots and tidy hair. Horses can of course be both unpredictable and inconsiderate. Being on the receiving end of a sudden earth-shattering sneeze or a nudge from a sweaty head won't do a lot for your personal grooming, but if you are wearing sensibly-coloured clothes (dark hues are generally best) you are more likely to survive the day looking reasonably presentable than if you are dressed in white.

If you are fortunate enough to look after horses that compete with an official team, you will probably be issued with a team uniform which you should always wear for official occasions such as inspections by the vets or parades or prize givings. Otherwise, make every effort to have neat, tidy clothes of your own for public occasions. An unkempt groom gives a poor impression, however beautifully turned out your horse may be!

Safety checklist

- Wear well-fitting, comfortable clothes that are easy to move around in.
- Avoid baggy garments that could become caught up on things around the stables.
- Always wear the safest footwear available that is also suitable for the job you are doing.
- Wear long sleeves to protect your arms.
- When wearing a coat, keep the buttons or zip fastened. A flapping jacket can startle a horse.
- If your hair is long, tie it back. Loose hair can become caught up and if it blows about on a windy day it can startle a horse.
- When buying waterproofs, choose 'quiet' materials, not crackly fabrics that can distract or frighten a horse.
- Never be tempted to ride in the wellington boots that you wear for mucking out, or in other footwear without safe soles and heels.
- When riding or lungeing always wear a hat, as recommended in *Chapter 1*, with the chin harness correctly fastened.
- Always wear gloves when lungeing, loading, and handling young or difficult horses.
- When riding over cross-country fences, or when schooling point-to-pointers or racehorses over hurdles, always wear a body protector.

Note for racing employees

In the racing industry it is the duty of trainers to ensure that their employees and agents wear correctly fitted and serviceable headgear at all times when mounted. Crash hats or riding hats are permitted provided that they are manufactured to BS 4472. Stable employees should never ride out with chin-straps unfastened, and the Jockey Club may take disciplinary action against a trainer whose staff do not comply with this regulation.

Index